Power of WOW! Customer Service

How doing what's best for the customer is best for the bottom line

Published in 2003 by Ron Morris Seminars
111 Makaroff Road
Saskatoon, Saskatchewan S7L 6R5
Canada
306-382-2639
www.ronmorrisseminars.com

National Library of Canada Cataloguing in Publication Data
Morris, Ron, 1950-

Power of wow! customer service: how doing what's best for the customer is best for the bottom line/ Ron Morris

Includes footnotes and index.
ISBN 0-9689434-0-3

1. Customer services 2. Customer satisfaction I.Title

HF5415.5.M68 2003 658.8'12   C2003-911220-9

Printed and bound in Canada by Houghton Boston Printers

This book is available at quantity discounts for bulk purchases
306-382-2639

This book is dedicated to:

Karen through thick (too little) and thin (too much) you always supported my dreams.

Without you this book wouldn't have been possible

Table of Contents

Acknowledgments

I would like to acknowledge the contribution of the following people:

My good buddy, Norm Rebin, who helped me believe that the world needed another good book on Customer Service. Your concern, encouragement, and constant stream of great humor kept me going.

My daughter, Robyn, for her excellent suggestions and for her early editing efforts that helped me to keep my structure and flow on track. Hopefully, you won't work that cheap your entire life.

Nicole Rebin, for giving me more insight over coffee on how to publish a book than I would have learned from reading fifty books. Thanks for saving me all that time, Nicole. I hope, at least, that I paid for coffee.

My editor, Jay Winans, of Blue Pencil, who, besides doing a masterful job, was also able to show me a thing or two about integrity. I look forward to working with you on the next project.

Last, but far from least, I have to acknowledge the ongoing efforts of my wife, Karen. You were all things to me during the production of this book—a computer guru, a part-time editor, a sometime slave driver, and a never-ending supporter.

Let's all do it again, real soon!

Introduction

Point of View

There was a time immediately following the Civil War, that a train was traveling from Charleston to Richmond. In one of the cars on the train there were four people. The first was an attractive young woman with dark flashing eyes. Her hair was as black as night. Her unlined, marble skin made it difficult to determine her age, but she was most likely in her late teens to mid-twenties. She had a trim figure, and a demure but attractive smile played about the corners of her mouth. She was the picture of a true Southern belle.

Seated beside the young beauty was her elderly and stern-looking grandmother. Her brow was perpetually furrowed, the corners of her mouth were downturned, and she was waiting, just waiting, for someone to give her an excuse to unleash her spite.

Directly across from the grandma was a stately old rebel general. Although his uniform was in tatters, dignity and grace emanated from him. His white mustache and goatee were trimmed to perfection. Not a hair of his full white mane was out of place. He was a man of substance.

Beside the general and across from the Southern belle slouched a handsome young Confederate lieutenant. His blond hair was long and unkempt and he had a mischievous glint in his eye. He was the kind of individual we wouldn't want our daughters to date.

A half-hour out of the train station in Charleston, the train entered a long tunnel. Fifteen seconds into the tunnel, there was a loud kissing sound, quickly followed by an indignant SLAP! Another twenty seconds passed, and the

1

train exited the tunnel. Everyone was seated as they were prior to entering the tunnel. Now, the characters were able to see one another's reactions.

The wrinkly, embittered grandmother was scowling at the lusty young man. She was thinking, "That impetuous young cad of a lieutenant! I knew he was trouble the minute I laid eyes on him. Imagine the nerve of him, kissing my granddaughter like that. At least I raised the girl well enough that she knew to give him a good slap! It serves him right! He won't try that again!"

The general sat with a look of confusion and hurt on his face, sporting an angry looking red welt. "What a terrible mistake has been made!" thought the general. "That young lieutenant of mine kissed that young lady, but she thought it was me. She hit *me!* She carries quite a wallop for someone so small!"

The young woman's face was flushed with embarrassment and perplexity as she pondered what happened. Both elated and disappointed, she thought, "That young man is a wonderful kisser, but my grandmother hit him so hard, he won't try to kiss me again when we're in the next tunnel."

And the young lieutenant, smug and satisfied, thought, "What a great day! How often do you get to kiss a beautiful woman and smack your boss *at the same time?!*"

It's a silly story, but it illustrates that in the upcoming pages everyone will be reading the same words but each finding a different meaning. We all come from different backgrounds, different geographical areas, and work in different industries. We even put different names on our customers. In the hospitality industry we call them guests, and in financial planning they're clients. Health care calls them patients, and in manufacturing, customers are called distributors. Airlines call them passengers. It doesn't matter, though, what we call them. They all have similar needs, wants, and expectations of the people that bring them Customer Service.

"Customer Service" means many different things to many different people. My company, Ron Morris Seminars, facilitates sales and customer-service training throughout North America in industries as diverse as those mentioned above, as well as telecommunications, oil and gas, publishing, and food processing There are differences, certainly, but there are more similarities. In this book my goal is to emphasize those common ingredients that will enable you to bring the Power of WOW! to your customers, no matter what title they go by.

Above all, though, Power of WOW! Customer Service recognizes that everyone brings their own perspective and history to a shared experience. Every one of us brings a different attitude to a shared experience. Customer Service is made up of complex relationships involving businesses, their customers, and their employees. Each of them takes away from a shared experience a different idea, conclusion, and attitude, just as the people in the Civil War story did. This book was written with the goal in mind that each party involved in a customer-service transaction comes away from the transaction feeling it was a positive experience, quite unlike what happened to the people in the Civil War story.

In order to accomplish this goal we should realize that the responsibility, the accountability, lies first, but not solely, with the business. There are, as expressed by Bill Guillory in his book *Spirituality in the Workplace,* two kinds of organizations: "Those where people count, and those where people don't count." The companies where people count are the type of companies for whom this book is intended. These are the companies that believe more in integrity than the bottom line. I have been fortunate to have had the experience of working for both types of companies, those with integrity, and those sadly lacking in that department. I was fortunate to work for *both* types because it gave me valuable insights into what makes one company flourish while another, no matter how much attention is paid to the bottom line, eventually flounders. I can tell you from personal experience, and show you in what will be proven later in the book statistically, that companies that hold integrity and respect in high esteem are the companies that are at the top of their industries. Earlier in my sales career at a brokerage firm, I was lucky to have a national sales manager whose favorite quote was "Take care of the customer and everything else will take care of itself." That was a valuable lesson for me, from an industry that is perceived to be only bottom-line driven. This book is very much about taking care of your customer first, whether that customer is an external or an internal customer. This book addresses the importance of planning how you will WOW! your customers. You will learn how to execute basic but vital customer-service skills. Don't buy this book if you expect to read it and magically have your customer-service challenges disappear. Implementing the skills and techniques you will learn in the following pages also requires patience and time.

Just as you shouldn't leave on a vacation without a map, you shouldn't embark on a customer-service program without a master plan. This book is your master plan for creating Power of WOW! experiences for your customers. As you take your customer-service journey, you will discover the importance of building customer loyalty and how to understand your customers' expectations in order to deliver more than they want. You will be able to set standards that will consistently place you as one of the most respected companies in your industry. You will learn how to build and foster a culture that will have highly talented people clamoring to work for your company. Your map will lead you to determine the huge upside in treating internal customers with the same appreciation and respect as you treat external customers.

This book provides examples of the skills and techniques that will set you and your company above others in today's competitive marketplace, skills such as how to become an active listener, and a technique that demonstrates how to deal confidently with an upset customer and arrive at a solution whereby both parties win. You will learn how to communicate with customers and co-workers alike in the manner that they would like to be treated.

What this book is:

If you're still reading the introduction, deciding on whether or not to buy this book, I can help you decide. In my many years as a salesperson, manager, and an entrepreneur, I have become a serious student of Customer Service. I have a good handle on what makes some companies excel and other companies flounder. Given that, I have created this book; it includes some of the best ideas about superior Customer Service from the best customer-service companies in the world. The book is filled with examples and ideas for skills and techniques that can set you and your company above your competition. There are exercises you can do to make your customer-service team more knowledgeable, more efficient, and cohesive. Besides that, it's priced right, and great value for the money. So buy it!

This book is also fun to read. You won't be bogged down by endless statistics, although some statistics have been used to support certain elements of the book. My goal was to keep the book light and accessible. You may find yourself smiling as you relate your personal experiences back to some of the scenarios in the book. There are places that you will laugh out loud. Fun is conducive to learning. Part of the problem with today's Customer Service is that we don't allow ourselves to have enough fun at work. Is it a coincidence that great customer-service companies like Southwest Airlines successfully make fun part of their customer-service culture? I didn't think so either. It's fun. So buy it!

Perhaps noted business speaker Zig Ziglar said it best when he stated, "If you will help people get what they want, you will get everything that you want." Doing this is easy to do. Why then, don't more companies do it? Because, unfortunately, it is just as easy not to do. Given the choice of doing what is best or doing nothing, although the difference in energy expended may be minimal, most will opt to do nothing.

What this book isn't:

This book wasn't written to make you believe that if you simply smile at your customers all else will fall into place. It isn't motivational. Education precedes motivation. Noted business speaker Jim Rohn says, "If you have an idiot, and you motivate him, you end up with a motivated idiot. And that can be hard to take." If you're still thinking of buying this book, that quote wasn't aimed at you. So buy it!

This book isn't inspirational either. I love to read those books when I want a burst of energy or a better feeling about mankind. This book won't take you to a higher plain of morality, but it will make you and your team excel at Customer Service. This book is not *Chicken Soup for the Customer-Service Soul.* It wouldn't be possible to accomplish in a publication like this what Mark Victor Hansen and Jack Canfield did with their Chicken Soup series, so you won't find stories that choke you up or bring a tear to your eye. Like the Chicken Soup series though, this book isn't hard to read. So buy it!

Purchasing this book means that you have already started on the road to Power of WOW! Customer Service. Purchasing this book means that you are willing to accept the huge responsibility of enhancing the level of Customer Service where you work, by committing to a program that is built on respect, integrity, and rewards built on simply what is best for your customers, be they internal or external.

SECTION I

ESTABLISHING

A

GOAL

Chapter One

Building Customer Loyalty: The Holy Grail of Customer Service

Why Are Loyal Customers Preferred over Satisfied Customers?

For years now companies have spent time, money, and energy on satisfying their customers. Why? A satisfied customer can be equated to a tie in a football game. Nobody loses, but nobody wins either. In his book *Customer Satisfaction Is Worthless: Customer Loyalty Is Priceless,* author Jeffrey Gitomer makes the point that customer satisfaction is the lowest rung on the ladder of success. If customer satisfaction shouldn't be our quest, then what should? The best way to build a business or work at a company that is enjoyable, meaningful, and profitable is to begin to build a loyal customer base from the outset.

The "how" of building a loyal customer base is important, but you shouldn't worry about figuring out "how" until you have mastered "why." Once the "why" becomes apparent, the "how" will get easy. If you are at all like me, you enjoy doing business with companies that enjoy doing business with you. These companies have employees that know your name, and your family members' names, and your favorite brands, and what size you wear, and on and on. This didn't happen by mistake. You have found one of the rare companies that recognizes that the reason to build customer loyalty is about more than the bottom line: it is about taking care of their employees, so that their employees enjoy coming to work and serving this cherished resource, the customer. It is about treating the customer with respect and care, so that the customer, like the employee, enjoys the interaction. The customer, in turn, will remain loyal to this company and its employees and will even tell their friends and family about the great experience they had in dealing with the company. If a company goes out of its way to treat you well, you will normally tell others. If on the other hand the company has great prices, it is usually the company that

11

will inform you, via some form of advertising, what a bargain it is dealing with them.

So what are the reasons that a company would want loyal customers rather than satisfied customers?

1. It's the Right Thing to Do

There are companies that exist just to make a profit. After all, that's why a business exists, isn't it?—to make a profit? If there is no profit, eventually there is no company. And these businesses have employees that work there, so they can take home a paycheck every couple of weeks. After all, that's why people work, isn't it?—just to make some coin? And these same businesses have customers who deal with them because the price is right, or they are in right area of the city. After all, these customers will remain loyal because the business has the right price or a good location, right? Well, no, actually. This is where we *see* it start to break down, but in fact the breakdown started when the company saw profit as its sole reason for being. You have been in this type of business. There is no joy, no laughter, and little respect shown between the parties, the business, the customer, and the employee. This is the type of business where the sales clerk tells you to "have a nice day" in their best monotone voice while looking out the window or trying to conduct a telephone conversation with a friend. This is the kind of business that is run with a 'bean-counter' mentality. More often than not, they will have strict policies and guidelines: "Note to all employees—you must wish the customer 'have a nice day.'" More often than not, the staff turnover is high, and correspondingly these companies are constantly on the hunt for new customers, because the old ones seem to have disappeared. There *is* a better way.

The flip side of this coin is to concentrate on doing what is best for the customer. This doesn't mean that you focus only on the external customer. Take pains to take great care of the internal customers, the employees, as well. Study after study has shown that companies that tend to kick around their internal customers have internal customers that tend to kick around the external customer. The external customer, not having to stand for that kind of treatment, chooses to take their purses and wallets to a different location that sells the same product, where they are treated with respect. The same studies show that companies that tend to treat their internal customers well, by treating them with respect, by allowing them some latitude in the customer-service process and keeping them informed as to the company's vision and direction, have internal customers that treat the external customer in the same manner. This makes for an experience where all three parties come away from any business interaction in a positive frame of mind.

2. Acquiring New Customers Is a Costly Enterprise

Studies have shown that it costs between four and seven times more money, effort, and energy to attract a new customer than to retain an existing one. Why is it, then, that so many companies pour thousands upon thousands of dollars into ad campaigns aimed at attracting new customers, while allowing their existing customers to vote with their feet and, more importantly, their wallets? Wouldn't it make more sense to spend more money, time, and energy on our existing clients? Ad campaigns are designed at attracting the customer who has yet to try the product.

3. Loyal Customers Refer Other Customers

Statistically speaking, a dissatisfied customer will tell eleven people of their negative experience, whereas a satisfied customer will tell seven.[1] Both of these numbers are on the conservative side in relation to other studies. We will explore some of the other numbers later in the book. Additionally, these numbers vary widely depending on the industry, but one thing is certain: whether you influence the customer in a

---

[1] U.S. Office of Consumer Affairs, "Complaint Handling in America: An Update Study, Part 2," T.A.R.P. April 1, 1986

positive or a negative way, that impact is leveraged. Have you ever stopped to consider the value of a customer who stays loyal to you for five years? One who spends, say, one hundred dollars a month. Most of us treat that customer like a one-hundred-dollar-a-month customer, which in most businesses isn't very well at all. If we project that same one hundred dollars until the end of the year, though, that customer is now worth twelve hundred dollars. Over the full five years, this customer is now worth six thousand dollars. They're starting to look a little bit better, aren't they? If you still aren't convinced that they are a valuable entity, let's assume that over the course of the years we really WOW!ed! them. We WOW!ed! them so much so that they sent us one referral at the end of each year, that spent as much or a little as them, depending on how you want to look at it.

Here's how that would look:

Value of a Loyal Customer Giving One Referral Per Year

Figure 1.1

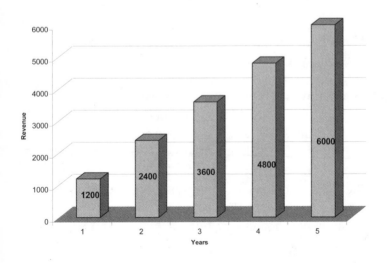

As you can see from Figure 1-1, by the end of the fifth year, your loyal customer is responsible for bringing six thousand dollars through the door for that year alone, simply by referring one person per year to your business, and has accounted for eighteen thousand dollars being spent at your business over that period. Do you treat that customer like an eighteen-thousand-dollar customer when they spend their average of three dollars a day? You can imagine what happens when you treat the people referred to you as well as you treated your original customer. Your business grows exponentially, your staff is challenged and busy, and your customers are happy to do business with you.

4. Settling for Satisfied Customers Is Settling for Mediocrity

The buzz words in the late 1980s and even well into the 1990s were *customer satisfaction.* Companies everywhere were falling all over themselves and each other to satisfy their customers. Wrong move. If you are able to satisfy your customers, congratulations on achieving mediocrity. That's all customer satisfaction is—mediocrity.

In the new millennium, the goal should be developing *loyal* customers. There's a huge difference. A satisfied customer base means that we haven't yet made them mad enough (or *dis*satisfied) enough to find another supplier of our products or services.

A loyal customer base, on the other hand, equates to a group of people that will go out of its way to deal with you on an ongoing basis. If I have a thousand satisfied customers and they march away to a competitor's doorstep, a potential disaster looms, because some will come back, and some won't. It's impossible to know how many will return. On the other hand, if a thousand loyal customers march away, I have no worries. If I have done my job and developed true customer loyalty, they will *all* be back.

Harley Davidson has it right as far as customer loyalty goes: if you can get your customers to tattoo the logo on their chest (or anywhere else!), that is true customer loyalty. A loyal customer base makes it easier to budget and to project cash flow, because those bumps in the road have been smoothed. We can predict with some degree of accuracy who will be purchasing which products from your organization in a given time frame.

> *"Loyalty today is no longer a function of rote or duty, but rather passion. You must do things so astonishingly well that customers become not merely loyalists, but rather apostles."*
>
> SkipLeFauve
> Chairman, Saturn

5. Loyal Customers Are Willing to Pay More

a) Profitability

When you deliver Power of WOW! Customer Service, price is not an issue. Loyal customers, because you are providing them with superior Customer Service and a high quality product, are willing to pay a premium to deal with you.

Companies that focus on delivering Power of WOW! Customer Service can charge higher prices because customers see the value, not just the price. As indicated in the Quality/Cost Relationship on the next page, if we see little value in the goods or services we are considering buying, the price seems astronomical to us. On the other hand, if the goods or services are perceived to be of outstanding quality, price becomes a less integral purchasing factor.

QUALITY/COST RELATIONSHIP

Figure 1.2

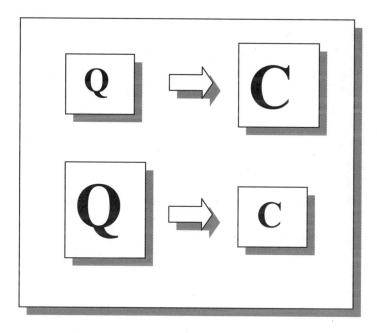

Allow me to illustrate this point with an example from my own history. There was a time, earlier in my life, that my clothing was poor quality. I had a habit of shopping at the "box" stores.

One day I was looking for a new suit. The one that I liked the most was relatively costly for my budget. I explained to the salesperson that I did a lot of traveling; my suits must be fairly wrinkle resistant. He assured me that the house-brand suit was exactly what I needed, and it just happened to be on sale. I made my purchase and looked forward to wearing my suit the very next day. I was due to make an important sales presentation in a city about two and a half hours away by car. Foolishly, I wore my shiny new blue suit, jacket and all, while driving. When I arrived at the office building where I was to deliver my presentation, I got out and checked how I looked in the mirrored exterior wall of the building of the company. I was aghast! Have you ever seen someone crumple a potato chip bag into a tight ball, then try to straighten it out? That's exactly how my shiny new blue suit looked—like a crumpled chip bag. Needless to say, my presentation wasn't as solid as it could have been, because I was sure that my audience was silently laughing at me. I *knew* that I looked foolish. I wore that suit only once after that, with the same result (I don't know what I thought would have changed!).

Although the suit didn't cost much compared to what I expect to spend today, the value wasn't there either. Consequently, the cost seemed too great. You would think that I would have learned from this experience, but there are days that I am not a quick study. Although I have never returned to that particular box store, I relived my poor judgment on quality by switching my clothing purchases to a different box store. Same stuff, different pile, or hanger, as the case may be.

The Quality/Cost formula didn't change. Every suit seemed to cost more than what it was worth. However, I was fortunate. At the second store, I had the privilege of meeting Terry Beaulieu, salesguy extraordinaire. He is the best I've seen in his field. He is knowledgeable and patient. He also has flair—the ability to put together an outfit that makes the customer look terrific, no matter the shape or size. He was in a league by himself, and on that inevitable day when he made the move to an upscale men's clothing store, I inevitably moved with him.

At his new store, Terry was quick to show me the importance of the Quality/Cost Relationship. "Sure the clothes cost more here," he said, "but your value is much greater. I invite you to give us a try. When you buy here, your clothing will be more wrinkle resistant and will last much longer." Terry was right on both accounts.

The rest, as they say, is history. Today, I buy all of my business clothing from Terry at Atch & Co., as well as the majority of my casual clothing. Do they compete with the box stores on price? Not really. Sure, they are competitive with other upscale men's clothing stores, but their thing is quality. Terry knows my name, my size, what my clothing has to do for me, as well as my color preferences and tolerances. Above all, though, Terry knows how to make me feel like I'm his number-one customer.

At year end, Terry offers a promotion called the Price Club. You simply pre-authorize your credit card or give a series of post-dated cheques for the year, and you can make your purchase for the year's total, plus a hundred and fifty dollars more, at any time. It makes buying easy. It means you use up your year's total early in the year. That means you will probably buy more later in the year. It means that price isn't an issue. Most companies wouldn't consider such a program. That's why I deal with Terry at Atch & Co. He brings quality to more than just the product.

Terry brings me the Power of WOW! because of the Quality/Cost Relationship, and because of this (it may sound warm and fuzzy, but it's true):

- ▣ **I give Terry referrals**. I just told *you* what great quality he offers, didn't I?
- ▣ **I am loyal**. I wouldn't consider buying my business clothing anywhere else.
- ▣ **I don't grind Terry on price**. In fact, I have such a great trust that he'll do the best possible for me, I rarely even ask the price.

By appealing to my sense of value, Atch & Co. is able to charge a reasonable amount for its product. Consequently, it is profitable and this enables it to introduce new lines and products on an ongoing basis.

Low-service/quality companies have a return on sales averaging just one per cent. High-service/quality companies have a return on sales of twelve per cent. That is a difference of eleven per cent. It means that high-service/quality

19

providers have a profitability more than ten times higher than their counterparts.[2] It also means that on a street somewhere in your town or city, a high-service/quality company is slowly picking away at the market share of a low-service/quality company. And one day, that low-service/quality company will be gone, because they weren't able to grow the business at a rate higher than their expenses.

b)   Revenue/Sales Growth

Everyone is willing to pay more, often substantially more, for what they perceive to be good Customer Service. An example I like to use in my seminars is the difference between shopping for groceries at a discount-style store as opposed to a "full-service" grocery store, such as Safeway. People seem to think that price is a major issue when we shop for something as fundamental as food. Admittedly, there is a segment of society that *has* to shop for food at a lower-end store, but why, then, would another segment of society *choose to pay more* for the privilege of shopping at a higher-end grocery store? After all, a quart of milk is a quart of milk, a pound of hamburger is a pound of hamburger, and a roll of toilet tissue is a roll of toilet tissue.

They choose to do it because full-service grocery stores do so much more:
- Bag the groceries for you.
- Don't charge you for the bags
- Have knowledgeable, friendly staff close at hand.
- Offer a "rewards" program.
- Have ample product on supply, even during huge sales events.
- Have parcel pick-up service for rainy or snowy days.
- Call you by name when you check out your groceries

---

[2] Jim Clemmer, *Firing on All Cylinders,* (Macmillian of Canada, Toronto, 1991) page 19.

Full-service grocery stores bring the Power of WOW! factor. Discount grocery stores bring the P.I.T.A. (Pain in the you-know-where) factor.

According to the Strategic Planning Institute, a worldwide non-profit group dedicated to the advancement of management strategy, companies that are perceived to be good service providers can charge ten percent more than companies that are perceived to be poor service providers. Imagine how your revenue stream would improve by just providing your customers with Power of WOW! Customer Service!

Customers who have had a negative experience take longer to pay. Not only does this affect your business's cash flow but it may mean that you have to hire a collection service, or in extreme cases, write the total off entirely. But wait, it gets worse!

What could possibly be worse than writing off the loss of a product or service that had a definite cost for you to provide? The person on the losing end of poor-quality service may feel the need to tell their friends and acquaintances about their lousy experience, rather than telling you. In fact, a study by TARP (Technical Assistance Research Project) found that, depending on the size of the purchase, only four to thirty per cent of unhappy customers even *bother* to lodge a complaint. These folks, although they may take longer to pay, have done you a big favor. They have brought to your attention a problem you may not have known you had. They are giving you a chance to make it right (see Recovery Standards, Chapter Three). The others are the kinds of people who would rather take their business elsewhere than fight with you. They do you no favors. They vote with their purses and their wallets. They leave you high and dry, mean-mouthing you all over town, giving you no chance to defend yourself.

That, my friends, will have a huge impact on your cash flow. It's like an iceberg. We see only the tip, those few that complain, but the real problem lies with the much larger base of the iceberg, the customers that don't complain. They simply disappear, never to return. The only way you may find out that a problem exists is from the complaints of dissatisfied customers that filter back to you secondhand via their friends, family, or co-workers.

c)   What's in it for me?

Still not convinced? Then maybe you should tune in to the most-listened-to radio station, WIIFM, What's In It For Me? No matter where you fit in the company hierarchy, taking care of customers just makes good sense.

If you are at or near the top, you recognize the positive impact that loyal customers bring to your bottom line. People that run companies are not only compelled by their job descriptions to be concerned with the bottom line but it is also in their very nature. A good many presidents and CEOs of companies are aware of a study that appeared in the September/October 1990 issue of the *Harvard Business Review* stating that a five-per-cent increase in loyalty will add from twenty-five to eighty-five per cent higher customer value, depending on the industry.

As companies flattened, downsized, right-sized, and in some cases capsized in recent years, no one group of people was as negatively impacted as middle managers. And yet I know personally of people in middle management who thrived in those years, because they had the loyalty of their staffs and customers. Creating customer loyalty as a middle manager means advancement and job security are yours to be had.

For those of you in an entry-level position, there's a good chance there will be increases in your take-home pay as you learn to bring more value to your customers as they deem it valuable. Most of us start at or near the bottom of the income ladder, at or close to the minimum wage of the land. The good news is that we have been issued a ladder, not a bed! If it were a bed, we would start at and remain at the same level. As we increase our value to our customers, though, their loyalty to us grows as our value to our employer increases. Building customer loyalty from an entry-level position is the fastest way to climb the income ladder. As I said, regardless of your position, no one will benefit more than you when you learn to develop a loyal customer base. It can be fun and rewarding to give great Customer Service. Making customers happy is a vocation; do what you love, love what you do! It takes the same amount of energy to supply a customer with a WOW! experience as it does to supply a ho-hum experience or a my-God-that's-awful! experience.

If you still can't buy in to the fact that Customer Service is important, let me assure you that there is still ample opportunity to set yourself above the competition by simply delivering superior Customer Service. All through the eighties and nineties we heard the customer-service mantras. As much as we spoke the words, we did precious little about it. Following are some surprising statistics that illustrate that no matter how much we talk about the importance of Customer Service, it seems that our customers don't agree.

Industry Customer Satisfaction Levels

Figure 1.3

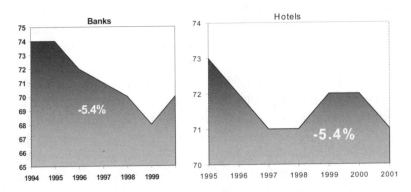

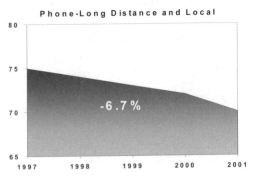

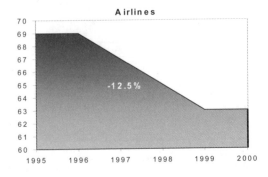

The graphs illustrated in Figure 1.3 demonstrate that for each of these selected industries, customer satisfaction has actually decreased rather than increased. Satisfaction with airlines has leveled off overall, while banks have actually shown a slight incline since statistics started being kept in 1995. Combined telephone, both local and long distance, have been in steady decline, and hotels, while showing some improvements for a short time, have once again started to head south. Could it be that companies haven't considered why customers come to them?[3]

Why Do Your Customers Deal with You?

Have you ever asked yourself this fundamental question? What makes your faithful customers, the ones that help keep your doors open, deal with you instead of your competitor down the street? I have come to believe that our customers deal with us for two reasons:

1) Our core competencies.
2) The level and quality of our Customer Service.

1. Core Competencies

Michael Vickers of Summit Learning Systems Inc. has developed an exercise that he does in his sessions to confirm that people do business with us for reasons other than just our core competencies. His exercise is described on pages 109 to 111 of his book *Becoming Preferred: How to Outsell Your Competition*. It's a powerful exercise that I have borrowed from Michael and that I love to do in my live sessions.

"Let's for a moment pretend that I have a pressing need for your product or service," I start. "It's in my best interest to undertake an investigation on who I should deal

---

[3]Diane Brady, "Why Service Stinks," *Business Week,* Oct.23, 2000: page 118.

with within the next couple of days. Like a lot of people, I want to get three quotes, and yours will be the first. Here is your chance to WOW! me. Tell me, why should I deal with you?"

Finding volunteers for this exercise is never hard. Every session I have ever done has at least one participant who relishes the opportunity to flaunt their product in front of a group. They must see it as free advertising.

For illustration's sake, let's assume that it is a fleet of cars we are dealing on. My volunteer will spew a list as long as your arm, with characteristics such as 'good quality,' and 'reliability.' Often times 'experience,' 'fair prices,' and 'a good reputation in the industry' will make the list. Every once in a while I hear 'great service' and 'we're in a great location.' I will put these answers on the white board or flip chart.

"Excellent!" I'll say. Great presentation." Leaving their answers visible, I will ask, "Could you supply me with the names of two of your competitors? What do you think they would tell me about buying vehicles from them?" Then I will point to the first word on their list of answers. If the word was 'good quality' they will counter with, "Sure, the competition might *tell* you that!"

If the next word pointed to is 'reputation' they will respond in the same manner. By the time I point to the third word, you can see light bulbs going on all over the room. I never have to ask about their second competitor, because they realize that the answers will be the same.

Why do I do this? Do I get a cheap thrill from embarrassing people? Not at all. I do it to simply illustrate that we can't differentiate ourselves, and we sure as heck can't build loyalty based on our core competencies alone. If our offerings are so similar to our competitors' offerings that they can't be told apart, in order to build loyalty we have to differentiate ourselves based on the level and quality of our Customer Service.

2. The Level and Quality of Our Customer Service
The best way to build a loyal customer base is through the efforts of your loyal customer-service team. So what hoops do you have to jump through to build loyalty in your staff? Read on. It's easier than you think, and very worthwhile. And appreciate that loyalty, like charity, begins at home.

The High Cost of Losing Business in Small as Well as Large Businesses

I used to use two different dry cleaners, one in my neighborhood and the other on the way to the downtown core where I conduct a lot of my business. The dry cleaner close to my home was a little less costly, but the term *Customer Service* was a concept foreign to them. They missed a beginner's basic of Customer Service, the fact that people's names are important to the owner of the name. My neighborhood cleaner, whom I would patronize at least once a week, would ask, "Name and phone number, please?" Their establishment was not so busy a spot that they couldn't remember my name after three or four visits. I frequented them faithfully, at least twice a week for about six months, and every time I was asked, by the same employee, no less, "Name and phone number, please?" Granted, some people aren't good at remembering names. If that's the case, write it down! How tough is that? "Plump guy with perpetually food-stained ties—last name is Morris."

The second dry cleaner eventually won all of my business. They did that by simply using my name and showing that they cared for me as a person. I dealt with the same person each time I took my clothing in, and after about three weeks, when I came through the door and plunked my clothing on the counter, I was greeted with, "Nice to see you, Mr. Morris. You need these tomorrow afternoon as usual?" WOW! This person had been paying attention. Now I go there at least twice a week, and I'm greeted by the same loyal, friendly, and enthusiastic employee. The only difference is that, now, when she sees me coming, my cleaning is already hanging on the hook by the counter, waiting for me when I arrive at the counter. I spend an average of thirty dollars per week with this company, or about $1,500 per year, just because a loyal employee showed me some recognition. The dry cleaner in my neighborhood became a pizza place not too long ago. Go figure.

In the hospitality industry, an industry that is plagued by high turnover, one company, Ritz Carlton, stands as a shining beacon of all that is right. Their people stay longer than those at most other hotel chains. They have a huge loyal client base. Why is that? It may start with their motto: "We Are Ladies and Gentlemen Serving Ladies and Gentlemen."

The motto demonstrates to the new employee that they are not just a number at Ritz Carlton. They are entering the company with a respected title, but with that title comes weighty responsibilities. There are twenty service basics that each employee learns, and perhaps none stands out so much to the new employees as number seven, which states, "To create pride and joy in the workplace, all employees have the right to be involved in the planning of the work that affects them". Not many companies understand the way to loyal customers is through committed, respected employees. Good on you, Ritz Carlton.

Building loyalty doesn't have to be a mystery. We have addressed the "why" of building customer loyalty in this chapter. How then, can we accomplish customer loyalty? The answer isn't as simple as you might hope or think. For every business in every industry in every town and city, there are so many variables that would lead to customer loyalty that no one book could begin to give you all of the right answers without knowing your situation or your customers' situation. How can you fix a problem when you don't know what the problem is? An old adage says that "if you don't know where you are going, any road will do." That's how it is when you set out to improve your Customer Service. You have to find out which road is the best for you. The first step towards building customer loyalty begins with Power of WOW! communications with your customers.

SECTION II

LAYING

THE

FOUNDATION

Chapter Two

Customer Expectations

> *"Nothing sets a person up more than having something turn out the way it's supposed to be, like falling into a Swiss snowdrift, and seeing a big dog come up with a cask of brandy around its neck."*
>
> Claud Cockburn

Any time we deal with a customer, one of three things can happen:

1) You can meet their expectations—no win, no loss here.
2) You can fall short of their expectations—they're miffed and tell a whack of people how lousy your service is.
3) You can exceed their expectations—you really WOW! them. They tell people too, just not as many. There is potential here to build customer loyalty.

Different studies have indicated that people who are dissatisfied with our performance will tell anywhere from fifteen to twenty people. People that were WOW!ed by our service will tell about half that number.

There are times when we forget that customers' perceptions are their realities. If they expect a great experience, and we provide what they perceive as only an adequate experience, we have fallen short of their expectations. On the other hand, if they expect adequate and we supply WOW!, we have exceeded their expectations and may be on the way to a loyal customer relationship.

Low Expectations, Great Result

My wife and I, though I love her dearly, often see the world through different-colored glasses. John Gray described this phenomenon well in his best-selling book *Men Are from Mars, Women Are from Venus.* The character of Norm on the eighties sitcom *Cheers* said it even more succinctly when he proclaimed, "Women: You can't live with them and pass the nuts." That summed up my attitude quite accurately prior to having a good deal of electrical work done during a recent home renovation. Karen, my wife, has dealt with electricians in her supervisory position where she works. She recommended a company by the name of Sommerfeld Electric, who I had heard of but knew nothing more. Hiring trades people should be a guy's domain, I thought. What would a woman know about hiring trades people? Admittedly though, my record has hardly been exemplary. I have hired people that showed up days after they promised, were under qualified, or didn't show up at all. Since I had no better recommendation, we decided to hire Sommerfeld.

The electrician was supposed to be at our home 'first thing.' What did that mean, I wondered? First thing after coffee? First thing in the afternoon? First thing after next weekend?

It was getting close to eight o'clock in the morning, and I decided to busy myself with a project since I was confident of not being disturbed by the electrician arriving before noon. Much to my surprise, the door bell rang at 7:58 sharp, and there stood Kevin, our electrician, looking very much like a person who was glad to be at work. He was neat, well groomed, and smiling like he had just run into a long-lost friend. My wife introduced us briefly before she headed out the door to work, and Kevin and I were left to tackle the job on our own. The first thing that I noticed about Kevin was that he removed his work boots in our home. I assured him it wasn't necessary, but he insisted. The second thing that I noticed about Kevin was the fact that when he wasn't stationary, working on an electrical outlet, he was running. He ran to the van to get a tool he needed, then he ran back to the house. He quickly removed his shoes and ran up the stairs. When he left for lunch, he ran down the stairs. When he worked, he hummed, whistled, or sang. This guy enjoyed his work! The job was completed about mid-afternoon, and Kevin asked where we kept the vacuum. I wasn't aware that we had a problem with the vacuum, but then I am from Mars. The next thing I know, Kevin was vacuuming his work area. He vacuumed the floor, polished fingerprints off of the new fixtures, and ran down the stairs to put on his shoes. Before running to his van, he thanked me for thinking of Sommerfeld Electric, and told me it was a pleasure to have met me. His grin was as wide as when he first arrived, and I couldn't help but believe he was sincere. I was WOW!ed. We have had more electrical work done since then, and each time we call Sommerfeld—who else would we call? We request Kevin. Every time he has come, he has exhibited the same degree of professionalism and energy as the first time. My wish is that every trade and every company took that same attitude to the marketplace. Unfortunately, that isn't the case.

Low Expectations, Poor Result

My wife and I were on a vacation recently in the pristine Canadian Rockies. We decided to dine at one of the newer hotels in the resort area. The hotel was well kept and had the advantage of a beautiful setting with craggy mountains disappearing into puffy white clouds as a backdrop. As we approached the hotel's restaurant entrance, I was a little taken aback by the handwritten sign that confronted me on the way in. It read: "We are not a fast-food restaurant. It takes time to prepare the meals. Your patience would be appreciated." It was signed "The Management." Granted, I don't get out much, but I am able to recognize a fast-food restaurant, and I knew, without being told, that this wasn't one.

Talk about changing my expectations! They were drastically lowered from the time we drove into the parking lot to the time we were seated. Before entering the restaurant, my expectations were to be treated to a tasty meal, a satisfying glass of wine, and friendly service at a reasonable price. Upon reading the sign, and seeing the restaurant almost totally full, my expectations transformed to, "My God, we'll be lucky to escape by midnight! I wonder how long these poor people have been here?" The management had, with a small 8½-by-11-inch sign, managed to redefine my expectations totally. Why not go all the way, I thought. Why not place another sign under the first, reading, "When your meal finally does arrive, you likely won't care for it." Perhaps a third sign could have been added at the bottom, stating, "Our speed and quality may not be very good, but our prices are out of this world!"

Since we had traveled a number of hours, and every restaurant in town appeared busy, there was no way we were leaving, forewarned of slow service or not! The sign had me on the lookout for any number of things to go wrong. And go wrong they did. The service, as promised, was slow. The server was friendly enough but obviously rushed. There were too many customers, too few servers. In years to come, I doubt this problem will persist! In mid-sentence, my appetizer was whisked away from the table faster than the speed of light, after it had taken two light years to arrive. The wine was too warm, the entree too cold. As suspected, the prices were out of this world.

My gut feeling told me that hiring and retaining competent staff at this establishment had been a challenge, and rather than fix the problem, the restaurant decided to squelch any complaints by apologizing for poor service in advance.

The point is this: highlighting your shortcomings will only serve to magnify any other problems your customers find with a service or product. In this case, the absence of a sign would have been a better idea. The sign lowered my expectations, but it also served to put my radar up to further problems.

A better way to handle the thorny issue of customer expectations can be summed up in two words:

1)   **Underpromise**
2)   **Overdeliver**

Rather than a handwritten apology prior to receiving lousy service, a happier ending to my story may well have gone like this:

Me: "It sure is busy in here tonight. What's the occasion?"

Server: "It's always like this. It's great to be busy, but sometimes it slows down service. In fairness to you, I should tell you that some of our patrons have waited up to a half-hour for their entrees."

Me: "Well, as long as I know, that shouldn't be a problem."

Server: "GREAT! Can I start you with a drink?"

Here's what happens when the entree arrives in twenty minutes, not the half-hour as promised.

Server: "They were able to get it out a little faster than I thought."

Me: " WOW! Very impressive."

It seems like a little thing, but underpromising and overdelivering are vital to managing customer-service expectations and perceptions. Make it a habit to promise a little but deliver a lot.

Moments of Truth

Every company, no matter the industry, will interact directly with their customers either face to face, through the electronic media, or through correspondence. These direct interactions are known as *Moments of Truth*. It is here that we have the opportunity to meet, fall short of, or exceed our customers' expectations.

Companies that excel at Customer Service are the companies most adept at handling their Moments of Truth. Moments of Truth present both challenges and opportunities. Customers will judge your business routines, product quality, and procedures. They may also reveal the next step to take in a relationship.

Some Traditional Moments of Truth

- A customer calls you, agrees to see you at their location, or comes to your location.
- The customer is angry or defensive.
- A customer has a unique request.
- Your customer can't make a decision whether or not to buy from you.
- A customer raises objections.
- The customer gives buying signals, such a asking more questions, leaning forward, or smiling.
- Your customer purchases what it is you are selling.
- The customer refuses to buy your product or service.
- A customer complains about your product, service, or your staff.
- A customer lets you know that they have been disappointed with some aspect of your service.

Delivering Power of WOW! Customer Service doesn't have to come from doing one thing many times better than your competitors it comes from doing many things just a little better.

1. When a Customer Appears, Acknowledge His or Her Presence

Even if you are tied up with another customer, let your new customer know that you appreciate their presence with a smile, a nod, or a wave. A verbal acknowledgment, such as "I'll be right with you," will also help.

2. Be Just as Polite and Prompt on the Phone

If the telephone comprises a big part of your business, make sure that your phone system is set up to handle the volume of calls. Many times, an incoming phone call is your potential new customer's first Moment of Truth with your company. Too many companies reward that first-time caller by exposing them to a rude, abrupt receptionist, known internally as Wilma the Grinch! You know the one—surly attitude, too quick to put you on hold or transfer the call, probably overworked, underpaid, and under trained. This is your caller's first exposure. Not a great start, is it?

Wilma the Grinch: "Acme Tools. Hold Please."

Potential new customer: "I don't have…"

(click, hold)

Or

Wilma the Grinch : "Acme Tools. Who would you like to speak with?"

Potential new customer: "I'm not sure. I was just calling about the advertised special on…"

Wilma Grinch: "The sales guys are all out. Call back later." (Click)

Do you think this doesn't happen? Believe me, there are leaders of companies out there that don't have a *clue* how their receptionist, their Manager of First Impressions, treats callers. The phone is still a powerful business tool. Make sure that tool is in the right hands!

My favorite companies don't use voice mail to answer the phones. They have a warm, pleasant voice to greet you. The best Managers of First Impressions will greet you, identify the company, themselves, and then offer to help you. It's about accountability, really. You are much more likely to hook a potential customer with a polite, friendly greeting, such as, "Good morning. Thank you for calling Acme Tools. This is Freda speaking. How may I direct your call?"

3. When a Customer Is Angry or Defensive

Above all, keep your head. If you are not in the wrong, don't use it as an opportunity to gloat. Even if you are (gasp!) wrong, there's no reason to lose your temper. Stand your ground and be proactive in problem solving. Empathize.

Listen—really, really listen. When emotions run high, our idea of listening becomes waiting for our turn to talk. Hear what the customer is saying. Try earnestly to understand what the customer is saying. Solve and close the incident smoothly. "Is there any other way I can help you today?" has a nice ring to it. It helps smooth ruffled feathers and soothe wounded feelings. Dealing with difficult customers is often the biggest stumbling block for people on the front lines. The ability to master dealing with difficult customers is such an important component of WOW! Customer Service that Chapter Seven is dedicated to this topic.

4. When a Customer Complains

This may sound unlikely, but it's in your best interest not only to welcome customer complaints but to increase your number of customer complaints. Complaints should be welcomed, because they bring your attention to what customers perceive as your shortcomings. If you don't know what's wrong with your service, how can you ever fix it?

Studies tell us that for every person who complains there are twenty-three who will vote with their feet and walk away from you and your business without making a sound. They don't argue, they don't complain. They will simply disappear. You may not even notice they are gone, until you look at your bottom line.

Take every complaint seriously. Even though a complaint may seem trivial to you, you must remember that the customers' perception is their reality. Treat each complaint, no matter how small it appears to you, with respect.

It's in your best interest to document and classify each type of complaint. This will help you to streamline your process. Not only will you be able to respond more quickly to the complaints, you can red-flag trouble spots and repair them. Try to consider complaints as constructive criticism from the people that really count: your customers.

Your business will improve if you treat each complaint as a learning opportunity. Ensure that your standards are developed internally so that complaints may be turned into opportunities.

5. When a Customer Is Unsure Whether to Buy from You

When a customer can't make a decision whether or not to buy from you, you want, first of all, to be sure that the person you are dealing with has the authority to buy from you. Earlier in my sales career, I was fooled many times, simply by dealing with people who had the authority to say no, but no authority to say yes. Here's the funny thing about people who don't have the authority to say yes—they won't tell you *unless you ask!* Ask politely if anyone else is involved in the buying process. If more than one person is involved, try to get all of them together at the same time.

Make sure you have a good grasp on your prospects' needs. Ask as many who, where, what, and why questions as necessary. Then listen closely to the answers.

If you are convinced that you're dealing with the correct person, and they still can't decide, you are likely dealing with a personality type that needs a little guidance. If that's the case, give this four-step process a whirl:

i. Make a recommendation for them.

ii. Justify the recommendation based on your perception of their needs. People buy on emotion, then justify their purchases with logic. If your justification inspires them emotionally and makes logical sense, you will likely have a buyer on your hands.

iii. Limit the number of options. There could be several options available to the customer, but limit your suggestions to two, possibly three. Too many choices will confuse and frustrate the indecisive buyer.

iv. Show confidence in your recommendation. Indecisive buyers respond well to firmness and confidence as long as the recommendation comes without pressure.

6. When a Customer Buys from You

This is the ultimate Moment of Truth. Your customer has shown enough confidence in you and your product to part with their hard-earned after-tax dollars. Buyer's remorse affects many people, no matter the product or its cost. As appealing as it may sound, now is not the time to take the money and run.

You have been presented with a golden opportunity to set yourself apart from the competition. Take advantage of it. A few simple steps will make your customers' decision to buy from you memorable for all the right reasons.

a) Assure them that they made the right choice. "You'll be glad you bought it!" is a great opener. Then, include some small token of your appreciation that the buyer wasn't expecting. It doesn't have to be huge; it just has to be more than they expect. For example, if it's a book, throw in a bookmark. For a computer purchase, a mouse pad would be nice. For larger purchases with good margins, such as automotive, engineering, or manufacturing purchases, the freebie can be more extravagant, like a shirt or cap with your logo. You will also want to write a letter the same day, assuring them that their satisfaction is your top priority. Mean it!

b) Follow up with a non-selling call. The line between sales and Customer Service is a little fuzzy sometimes, and it's hard to see which functions belong to which component. I have come to believe that sales and Customer Service are linked inextricably, and that the best salespeople, no matter the product, offer the best Customer Service.

Too often the only time our customers hear from us is when we want to sell them more of our goods. How cheesy! Your customers will be WOW!ed by the fact you're calling just to see if the purchase is performing to their expectations, if they're satisfied with it, and if they can think of ways you can serve them better.

c) Stay in touch, and make use of journal responses. Learn your customers' buying cycles, the beginning of their yearly budgets, and be knowledgeable enough about their business and industry to know when opportunities may arise. Keep a record of all of your conversations, either on paper or electronically, and be there for your customers when you're needed.

d) Make your customers champions of your cause. Nothing sells like a satisfied customer. Don't hesitate to ask your happy customers for reference letters and referrals. They will be glad to share in your success. Get reference letters from as many regions and industries as you can.

If your customer wants to help with a letter but doesn't know what to say, offer to write the letter on their behalf. Some people won't be happy with this arrangement. Make the process easier for them by giving them a choice of three styles of letters.

The first letter should be very understated. It will state that you are adequate, but no more. Make it sound like nothing really terrible will come from doing business with you.

The second letter will be written in the exact words you want to see written about you, without going overboard. It can speak to your credibility, your helpfulness, and your knowledge. Don't embellish so much so that your customer is uncomfortable with the theme.

In the third letter, though, embellish all you want! In this letter, you can claim to be the greatest thing since sliced bread. You are witty, articulate, attractive, and have just saved helpless children from a burning building—well, not quite, but you get the picture.

Now give your customer the choice of the three letters, written on their letterhead. Which will they choose? Invariably, they'll pick the second letter. The first one will make them feel too cheap, too chintzy with their praise, but the third letter is too effusive. They like you and your service, but not *that* much. So, the second letter it is. That's the letter you wanted to see in the first place. Everybody wins.

Depending on your product or service, you will have a variety of opportunities to exceed your customers' expectations. To help you determine where your opportunities lie, we have included the Moments of Truth Circle (Fig. 2.1) with some more examples of Moments of Truth.

As a quick exercise, record your company's Moments of Truth. You will likely come up with more than twenty-four. Under each of your Moments of Truth, leave a space of about three or four lines. In this space, record where you can provide Moments of WOW! in your customer-service circle. If you have really progressive ideas, you may need more space. That's great! This process is labor intensive, but if you are able to involve the entire team, you will be pleasantly surprised as to how many WOW! ideas come out of it.

Moments of Truth Circle

Figure 2.1

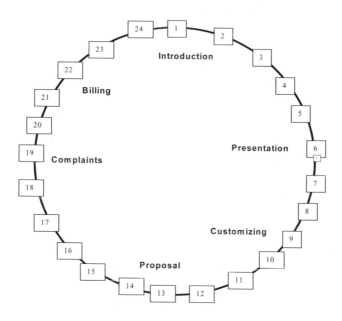

MOMENTS OF TRUTH CIRCLE

1. Initial incoming phone call from customer
2. Call is transferred or ended with message taken
3. Company representative phones customer
4. Company representative goes to customer's place of business
5. Company representative does presentation
6. Customer raises objections
7. Customer has special requests
8. Customer gives buying signals
9. Customer refuses to buy your product
10. Customer becomes angry or defensive
11. Company representative sends quote via fax, e-mail, or regular post
12. Company representative presents quote at customer's place of business
13. Customer visits company representative
14. Customer agrees to purchase your product
15. Customer needs it NOW!
16. Customer changes initial order
17. Company representative delivers order
18. Customer exhibits disappointment with some aspect of the order
19. Customer complains
20. Company representative apprises customer of problem with order
21. Company representative follows up
22. Company invoices customer
23. Company sends statements to customer
24. Company places collection call to customer

There is a lot less heartache (and a lot happier workplace) when you know what the customer expects of you. It is similar to going to a fast-food outlet for a meal. A Big Mac or a Whopper or a Teen Burger gives the same experience whether purchased in Minneapolis, Sydney, or Vancouver. That is because the people that run these companies have established a consistent set of criteria that gives the customer a level of comfort, since they know what to expect in the way of way of food ingredients, signage, and furnishings from one part of the world to the next. This set of criteria is known as *standards.* Standards are the measurement by which your customers judge your service. Standards are like a bar that is constantly being raised. As the bar, or minimum acceptable standard, is raised, your customers will expect more. If you value their loyalty, you must once again raise the bar or refine your standards upwards.

Chapter Three

Establishing Standards

Right Process, Right Result

Picture this: you are driving to an important appointment when you feel your car pulling strongly to the right. You pull over to see what's wrong. Your worst fears are confirmed. The tire on the front passenger side is flat. Being the prepared individual that you are, you believe you have all the necessary tools with you. You also know that if you fix it quickly, you will still make it to your appointment on time.

Quickly, you go to your trunk, and you're relieved to find that all of your tools are still there. You put the jack on the ground, jacking the car up as high as you can as fast as you can. You remove the hubcap and try to take the flat tire off. Much to your dismay, it just spins. And spins. And spins. No matter how hard you try, no matter how much pressure you apply to the lug nuts, the tire just continues to spin. How can that be? You have all of the right tools. The problem is that your process is flawed. Wrong process, wrong result. Now if you let the car back down so the wheel touches the ground, it's easy to remove the nuts. You change the tire, and are back on our way. Right process, right result.

Changing a tire is no different than Customer Service. If you have the right tools and the right process, your Customer Service will have the Power of WOW! If you have the right tools, and the wrong process, you've already seen what happens. It just won't work.

The formula that we call the Customer Service Success Formula goes like this:

S₊TₓEx₌POW!

$S + T_x E_x = POW!$

S = Standards

T = Teamwork

Ex = Execution

POW! = Power of WOW!

Let's look at each one of these on its own to see how it best fits our process.

Standards

Standards are our road map for building customer loyalty so that we can deliver Power of WOW! Customer Service. Standards are easy to develop, but not so easy to live by.

From FedEx to Marriott Hotels, from Dell Computers to Nordstrom's, the great customer-service providers all have one thing in common: ambitious yet attainable standards on how they treat their customers. Standards help to set customer expectations and train your staff to be effective. Brian Tracy of Peak Performance says that the biggest problem in the North American workplace is that employees don't know what's expected of them. Well-defined standards make that little problem disappear.

Here's the deal, though: You can't set your standards until you know what it is your customers think or feel about your products or services. Put yourself in your customers' shoes and determine what their stresses are. Then, using this book as your map, set up processes to eliminate those stresses.

Process, process, process. Even setting standards is a process that should look like this:

1. Identify Customers' Expectations

What do your customers expect in the way of reliability? Responsiveness? Empathy? What do they expect of your company's tangibles, your locations, the appearance of your company vehicles, equipment, and employees? How many rings do they expect it will take you to answer the phone? How do they expect to be greeted? Your customer has an expectation on all of these things and a lot more.

Our first step in the standards process is to find out what those expectations are. The easiest way to do this is to make a list of what you expect from businesses that you deal with, in both your business and personal life. Make a note of what makes you grit your teeth and clench your fists when you deal with a company. Things like employees that share with co-workers the details of last night's date while you are at the checkout, or companies that never have advertised specials in stock, or invoices that are never right. Some companies make me grit my teeth because they have poor hours of service or a location that is unusually difficult to get to or to find. They may answer their phone in a rude manner, or not until it rings five times. Whatever your teeth-gritting list is comprised of, don't follow that model! Now, make a note of the companies that make you say WOW! when you deal with them, no matter what industry they are in. There is the start of how you model your Customer Service Process. If we have high expectations as customers of other companies, you can bet that our customers have the same expectations of us.

Here's a challenge for you during this exercise. Write down the name of five companies that deliver the Power of WOW! when you buy from them with your personally hard-earned, after-tax dollars. You know the types of company— the one that really gives you a warm, fuzzy feeling when you pay the bill or get that follow-up phone call. The kind of company that really makes you say WOW! This can be anyone you deal with. Maybe it's your automotive dealer or mechanic. Perhaps your travel agent or grocer makes you say WOW! when you deal with them. How about a hairdresser, bank, jeweler, or clothier?

I ask this question of business people in attendance at my customer-service workshops across the country. It's rare that anyone comes up with five, so don't feel atypical if you couldn't identify that many. I'm constantly amazed, though, at the people who can't even come up with one company that makes them say WOW! Here's a scary thought: if we can't think of one, what are the chances that our customers are saying WOW! about us?

2. Set Your Standards

Once you know what it is your paycheck (customer) expects, set standards that are just a little better. That's the beauty of great Customer Service. You don't have to be ten times better at things to be ten times more successful than your competitors, ten times more profitable than your competitors, or have relationships that are ten times better than your competitors. You simply have to do the little things as good as or a little bit better than your customers expect.

Once you have your standards in place, make sure that you monitor them against your actual transactions. If this reflects good business practice, congratulations, you have a winner! If not, modify your standards. You still want your standards to be hard to reach, but not so much of a reach that they are unrealistic or unattainable.

We could start a debate here: should you compare yourself to industry standards or forge your own path? If you aren't concerned with your competitors, how do you know how you compare? It's simple—don't worry about the competition. I have come to learn that the great companies make their own way in the world. You won't find them looking over their shoulder to see who may or may not be gaining. If you set your own rules, then set your own ambitious standards, and live by them. Soon enough, the rest of your industry will be chasing you!

3. Develop Consistency

Okay, you have the start of a process in place. Now that our standards are set, never, never, never, deviate from those standards! I cannot emphasize this enough. Your standards are your business bible. Everyone in the organization should be as aware of your standards as they are of your Mission Statement. They *are* familiar with your Mission Statement, aren't they?

The key to consistency is that your standards are *measurable.* You may hear from some of your staff that what they do can't be measured. Be wary of these people. In most cases, they don't want their performance to be measured because they may be found wanting. You may hear from some of them, "Sorry boss, but you just can't measure friendliness." Maybe so, but you can measure the components of friendliness. You can make it a standard that all customers are greeted with a smile, whether on the phone or in person. You can make it a standard that staff maintain eye contact with customers. You can standardize the way you greet callers on the phone. For example: "Thank you for calling Acme Acne Cures, this is Melanie. How may I direct your call?" Yes, it's a friendly statement, but it is also precise and measurable. That exact phrase, if used on a consistent basis, becomes a greeting standard!

You can make it a consistent standard that employees use customers' names a certain number of times in a conversation. Even parting, such as, "Thank you for coming in," can be a standard. Is it friendly? Yes. Is it measurable? Yes.

Standards have to be consistent to be effective. They also have to be specific. It's a bit like goal-setting. "I want to be rich" is not a goal, whereas "I want to retire on September 30, 2005, with two million dollars in my retirement fund, and have a net worth of three million dollars on that date" is a specific, measurable goal. There's a big difference between the two. It's the same with Customer Service. Rather than state "I want to offer good Customer Service," a statement such as "I will ensure that customers are greeted with ten seconds of entering my establishment" or "I will ensure that all components of our billing process, including costs, addresses, and spelling of names are one hundred per cent accurate." The more focus we give to an area of Customer Service, the more measurable it becomes. The chances of that standard being met increase significantly.

Here are some examples that start as good service quality but can be transformed into specific, measurable customer-service standards.

Good Quality	Specific Standard
Answer phone promptly	Answer the phone within three rings
Answer the phone in a friendly manner	Answer the phone with, "Thank you for calling Aardvark Insurance. Bob speaking. How may I direct your call?"
Make your customer interactions memorable	WOW! a customer per day by sending a thank-you card for a good meeting or for doing business with you
Be accountable for helping the customer	Always give the customer your name and pertinent contact information
Show the customer that you care	Greet the customer by name if you know it. Make eye contact within three seconds of being approached

Standards can make or break your customer-service process. It's in your best interest to give standards the attention that they deserve. Standards are also more meaningful and more powerful when they are created in collaboration with management and staff. Please don't make the mistake of thinking that because you are in management that you necessarily know what's best for the customer. Your front-line people in the trenches are your second-best source of what the customer wants. (Number one would be your customers themselves. Unfortunately, customers aren't often asked what they want.)

Your people are your most valued asset (most companies say this, but few live it). They can supply you with a wealth of information. They are the first to hear the complaints, needs, and desires of your customers. They hear what your company does right and where things could be improved. It makes sense that your team should have substantial input on developing your standards. We will look in depth at how you can create a happy and loyal front line in Chapter Five. A satisfied and loyal front line is imperative if you are to capitalize on the next component in the success formula:

Teamwork

> *"An automobile goes nowhere unless it has a quick, hot spark to ignite things, to set the cogs of the machine in motion. So I try to make every player on my team feel like he's the spark keeping our machine in motion. On him depends our success."*
>
> Legendary football coach Knute Rockne

Whether your teams are specific departments within a large organization or a group of employees dedicated to accomplishing the same task in a smaller organization, there is one constant: teams need a compelling vision to act as their compass. This will act as their guide, not only when they are on familiar ground but especially when they venture into new territory.

Make the company's vision—your mission—known, and explain clearly how their contribution is valued. A few years back I did a customer-service training session for a small company that had a very noble mission. I introduced the topic of the company's vision, and to his dismay, only the president and one long-term employee really knew the mission. The company, WPD Ambulance was in the health-care industry, and the president, a man who cared deeply about his team, was amazed and disappointed. Being a person of accountability, he took it upon himself to address the oversight immediately, and we extended the session to address the vision. Today, learning the company vision is new employee's indoctrination to the company. He explains how their commitment to the team contributes to the overall vision of the company.

Some companies that I have worked with have gone as far as encouraging individual departments to develop their own vision. As long as their vision is in lockstep with the company's vision, this can be a powerful tool.

There are other variables that will contribute to a team's success, many of which are discussed in detail in Chapter Five (Happy Employees = Happy Customers). Following are what I feel are the four most important things you can do for your team to show them that you care.

1) Give them pertinent information
Withholding information from them may make you feel as if you have total control. The opposite will happen. They will think that they don't have your trust or your confidence. That's how 'us versus them' starts.

2) Be inclusive

Don't just let them know what has been decided. Share the 'why' as well. Like any relationship, good teamwork is built on trust, and this will go a mile to developing that most important ingredient. It's best to do this face to face and one on one, if at all possible.

"That's my decision, and it's final!" smacks of authoritarianism, and won't garner much of a buy-in.

3) Teach a man to fish...

Don't make it a habit to scurry in and 'save the day' when they encounter early problems. Give them guidance, certainly, but the power in teams is letting them grow in knowledge and confidence as they overcome obstacles in their way. Accept that mistakes will happen. If you continue to feed them rather than teach them, they will learn to count on you when the going gets tough. It's true that people learn from their successes. They also learn from their failures.

4) Trust them to make the right decisions

Studies have shown that the strongest message that management can make is to support their teams. Give them leeway, give them power, give them confidence. Some of the world's most innovative companies encourage their teams to make decisions on other team members' performances.

5) Say what you'll do, and do what you say

Team members are quick studies, and they will spot inconsistencies in a minute when they compare what management says to what management does.

One of the greatest proponents of Customer Service that I have had the privilege to know is Jim (Truckload) Turner. A large, gregarious man, blessed with an offbeat sense of humor and a firm commitment to his teams, taught me one of my most memorable customer-service lessons. Now the owner of a successful grocery store, he started with the chain he is now with as a department manager. It wasn't long before his retail talents were noted, and he was elevated to the position of store manager.

The viability of the store was tenuous at best, and there was talk of the chain closing the store. Now one of Turner's favorite sayings was "My door is always open." He said it with a huge grin on his face, and a twinkle in his eye, but he meant it from the bottom of his heart.

The day came when the suits from head office came to town to discuss with him the store's potential closing. Being a sensitive issue, they closed the office door. Without a word, Turner got up and opened the door. Again they closed the door. This time Turner explained his position and what he had said to his staff. Their stance was that this was far too sensitive an issue to discuss in the open. A somewhat heated debate took place, but in the end the meeting took place with the door closed.

The folks from head office won this round. When the meeting ended, the taillights of the car were still visible when Turner retrieved his hammer and screwdriver from his toolbox. He removed the door and took it to his home, where it stayed until he was promoted to the next challenge.

On his return to the store he gathered the staff and announced merrily, "It's back to normal. My door is always open!"

The store didn't close; in fact it turned around and is a viable entity. Truckload Turner went on to solve other challenges as a manager in other locations before being offered ownership in his current location.

The most important thing to come out of that episode, though, was that the team saw a commitment from their manager to them. It was a memorable, meaningful lesson. The store, a union operation, had been mired in petty grievances. From that day forward, that ceased to be a meaningful issue. Walk the talk, and your teams will take notice.

Execution

This entire book is about how to execute a successful customer-service plan. I would like to touch on it here briefly in order to give you an idea as to how it fits into our overall goal of Power of WOW! Customer Service.

Execution is likely the most important component of the Customer Service Success Formula. Predictably, most companies can figure out the Standards and Teamwork components. "Aha!" they holler. "Now for the easy part. We'll develop a catchy slogan that our internal and external customers will buy into, and we will become customer-service legends!"

Just as predictably, this is where it all starts to go south. How can that be? We have determined what our customers need and want. We have the systems and the team in place, and they are well trained. So, why isn't this working like it's supposed to? Why are customer complaints just as prevalent? Why isn't our business growing like we were told it would?

The reason is that you are providing lip service, not Customer Service. Not less than ninety-one per cent of businesses claim to have a customer-service theme, a customer-satisfaction program, or a customer-focused training program in place. The problem is that most of these companies fail in their execution of their plan.

In the United States, only sixteen per cent of companies feel that they have reached their customer-satisfaction goals.[4] Not only do companies fail to WOW! their customers, for the most part customers do not find doing business a "pleasant buying experience." The very sad part of all this is that the eighty-four per cent of companies

---

[4]Deborah B. Taylor, "The Missing Links of Customer Satisfaction," *How to Really Deliver Superior Customer Service,* (edited by John R. Halbrooks, Inc Publishing, 1996) page 18.

that don't make the grade, *know what to do*. They even know *how* to do it. They just don't do it.

How many times have you phoned a company, only to let the phone ring six or seven times before you give up, thinking that you dialed incorrectly? You promptly re-dial, and the phone is answered on the fourth ring. If you are like me, one more ring and I would have assumed that the company I was calling was:

a)   Out of business, or

b)   Far too busy to deal with me.

This happens frequently. This is an example of a company that hasn't bothered to set an incoming-call standard. If they are ignoring that oh-so-important first impression, in what other areas are they weak?

Our ability to set, maintain, and surpass standards will ultimately determine if our Customer Service is fantastic, flop, or fiction. Companies that set ambitious standards, and are then able to consistently deliver those standards, are the companies that deliver Power of WOW! Customer Service and have loyal customers that in many cases will become downright advocates.

According to Kristin Anderson, standards are "the rules you write for getting work done." The number of standards you set is up to you. One thing is clear—common sense should prevail. You can go wild setting standards for everything from soup to nuts. Most companies that are perceived to be successful at delivering Power of WOW! Customer Service will have between eight and twenty sets of standards. Every industry, every sector, has its own set of standards.

The standards you set should fit like a fist in a glove for your company. Develop too many and you won't be able to keep track, and they will lose meaning and credibility. Develop too few and yours will become an organization that is run by the inmates, where customers are as rare as dodo birds.

Developing Standards

If you can get a buy-in from your team as you develop standards, all the better. The standards that have the most power are developed by the team at large. Get everyone—yes, everyone—in your organization to contribute during a live meeting. If your company is too large to have everyone together in one place at the same time, at least make sure that every department has representation. The greater the sense of ownership, the greater the chances of your standards being adhered to.

Have everyone, time permitting, introduce themselves and give a brief explanation of what they do. Break into groups, and make sure that no group is dominated by a single department or division.

Next, using flip chart paper or a white board, have a staff member or a professional facilitator introduce a number of key areas in which you want to set standards. You can draw on some of the standard examples on the following pages, such as feedback and recovery standards, or possibly client communication standards. You may be in an industry where you have standards peculiar to your industry or company, like response-time standards with protective services, or cleanliness standards in the hospitality industry.

Everyone should have input as the standards are developed. Unless you have regular meetings where every department has a chance to interact with other departments, you will be surprised at the reactions. You will almost be able to see light bulbs going on over people's heads as they realize that what they do affects other departments and how they contribute to the big picture.

This is a great opportunity to include a couple of team-building exercises and to weave this session around a staff-appreciation event. At one seminar a woman came up to me at the completion of just such a session and said, "I have been a part of this organization for almost two years and today is the first time that I really felt a part of it. Now I have an appreciation for what everyone else has to go through, and I see exactly how my contribution helps."

The diversity of the groups becomes a great learning tool for everyone involved. It's a good idea to start with only your top five or six standards, the ones you couldn't exist without. Here are a few that I feel every organization should have:

1. Feedback Standards

How are you going to set standards if you don't know what your customers want? Often we are quick to assume that we know what's best for our customers because we just spent countless hours developing a great new product. Since we haven't yet seen sales plummet, we think that our existing products are doing fine, just fine.

Sorry, it doesn't work that way. Every product or service we deliver should be subject to feedback standards. We should always be taking our customers' pulse to find out how we're doing right here, right now, as well as determining their ongoing expectations.

Feedback can be garnered in two ways:

a) Learn to ask great questions
b) Survey your customers regularly

Let's take a close look at these options. Both methods are effective, and both can save you some heartache. The last thing you want to bring to the marketplace is another Edsel. Are you old enough to remember the Edsel? It began production in 1957, and that year introduced its 1958 model, a revolutionary, much ballyhooed vehicle. The Ford Motor Company spared no expense in promoting it. Two-page ads were procured in *LIFE* magazine. They bought the time slot of the mega-popular *Ed Sullivan Show* on Sunday, October 13, 1957, to promote their new car. The show, entitled "The Edsel Hour," was hosted by the top performers of the day:

Frank Sinatra, Bing Crosby, Louis Armstrong, and Rosemary Clooney. The show had *huge* ratings. Everyone watched the show; nobody bought the vehicle.

Enormous sales were predicted for the car, but it's distinctive front grill design prevented all but a few from actually making a purchase. The car touted to be one of the best-selling vehicles of all time was in production for barely two years. It was a bust. Big time. Why? No one knows. Certainly, Ford doesn't know. And they don't know simply because they didn't ask. In their zeal to honor Edsel Ford and introduce a revolutionary product to the marketplace, they forgot to consult with the buying public.

What Ford did was introduce the equivalent of a better mousetrap. If you're going to build a better mousetrap, first make sure that the world wants a better mousetrap. Here's how:

a) Learn to Ask Great Questions
Ask questions that will let you know what's bugging your customers. A simple yet telling way to find your customers' expectations is to ask them where they like to shop.

? Great question #1
"What's your favorite store?" or "Where do you think/feel you get the best bang for your shopping buck?" is sure to generate a little conversation with a customer that you know fairly well.

Listen closely to the answer. It will give you an insight into what the customer perceives as quality (or even WOW!) service. The next question is even more important.

? Great Question #2
"Why?"

Listen even more closely to this answer. It will tell you not only what the customer deems valuable, it will also reveal what the customer expects. Once you have this information, you can go about applying the same level of service, plus a little more, to the products or services that you provide this same customer. Another great question should be asked of yourself.

? Great Question # 3

"What is the unmet need?"

One seminar I attended a few years back had a Ken (of Ken and Barbie fame) type of presenter. His favorite theme was, "There are no problems, only opportunities!" At the time, this seemed ludicrous to me. No problems? Who is he kidding? My working life was full to the brim with problems. It took a while for the light bulb to go on over my head, but eventually it did. Ken (if that was his real name) couldn't have been more right! My sales took off when I came to realize that I wasn't selling a product, I was in fact solving problems for presidents of companies, vice-presidents of sales, sales managers, and human-resource professionals. They all had one thing in common—they had needs that weren't being met. Suddenly, the world seems full of opportunities. Before the light bulb went on, though, I had to realize where the shortfalls were in the training market. The unmet need in my industry was ongoing training. Lots of training organizations would go into a company for a short period of intense training, then they were gone in a lightning flash. Companies were tired of the sunburn effect. In our programs we meet extensively with the company prior to the training, enabling us to customize a solution for the client that is based on a stress that they are encountering. Then we built their specific program, delivered it, and offered follow-up sessions to ensure they *got it.*

One of the best stories I heard about recognizing an unmet need revolved around a lady by the name of Bette Nesmith. In 1951, she was a recent divorcee and single mom who was struggling in her job as executive secretary at a bank. The main source of her frustration was a new-fangled invention, the electric typewriter. It was too fast, there were too many typos, and the frustration mounted for Bette. In an attempt to hold onto her job, she produced a magic potion of a water-based paint and coloring agent that blended with the bank's stationery. This new correction fluid worked so well, that Bette's co-workers started asking for it. She started to bottle it and sell it. By 1956, sales were good enough to support Bette as she operated out of her garage.

Let's flash ahead to 1979, when the Gillette Company bought Nesmith's Liquid Paper Corporation for $47.5 million.[5]

Nice work, Bette. It all stemmed from an unmet need.

Even Michael Dell, one of the great marketers of our time, nearly blew himself up in 1989. Dell Computers developed a product so powerful and so broad, they were sure the buying public would buy it. It was code-named Olympic, and Dell was convinced it would lead them on "a huge wave of growth." Luckily, before it reached market, they started telling some of their customers about it, even if it was a little late in the game. No one was impressed. At least, not suitably impressed enough to buy the product. So the project was canceled without having seen the light of day. Said Michael Dell of the experience, "if we had consulted our customers first about what *they* needed—as we had been accustomed to doing—we could have saved ourselves a lot of time and aggravation."[6]

b) Surveys
Surveys are the most common means of generating customer feedback. Before you start to implement changes to your customer-service processes and standards, first ask questions of existing and past customers. The best place to start,

---

[5] Michael LeBoeuf, *How to Win Customers and Keep Them for Life,* (Berkley Pub., New York, 1987) page 60.
[6] Michael Dell, *Direct from Dell,* (HarperCollins, New York, 1999) p.39.

though, is right at home. Have a look at your own staff to find out how they feel about working where they do. Let's be honest. There are times when it is better to terminate an employee than try to save their job. It may be a case of having conflicting values, or you may have an employee with a great attitude, but a poor work ethic. Maybe the challenge is reversed—their work ethic is fine, but they can't relate to customers or co-workers without a great deal of tension. Either way, your job is not to save the world but to generate great results through Power of WOW! Customer Service. If an employee doesn't fit with your culture, you're doing them a favor by having them move on.

If staff turnover or morale are issues, jump all over this type of survey. You may be surprised to find that the problem lies with you, not your staff.

▣ Employee Surveys

You will want to ask questions that identify how satisfied people are with their positions. What do they think of communication within the company? Is it honest, two-way communication or does it come from the top down, offering employees no opportunity for feedback? Do employees have a sense of teamwork and satisfaction with their jobs? It's a good idea to have employees rate their supervisors.

Survey Method: Confidential written questionnaire.

▣ Random Surveys

This type of survey is used to measure overall customer satisfaction and to red-flag certain aspects of your service. This is a great starting point if you haven't previously surveyed your customers. Pick a percentage of your overall customer base, and go for it. You should consider yourself fortunate if you have a response rate of over fifty per cent

Survey Method: Telephone, mail, or in person. You may want to combine any two or all three of these methods to ensure you get at least a fifty per cent response rate.

▣ Key Account Surveys

The Pareto Principle lives! Most of us will derive roughly eighty per cent of our incomes from about twenty per cent of our customers. It makes sense that we do our best to get close and stay close to these people. Just by asking for their input shows your key account clients that you truly care about their business. If you purchase services or products from a company partly because they show you personal attention, the same would apply to your clients.

<u>Survey Method</u>: Telephone, in-person, or focus-group discussion.

▣ Lost Account Surveys

These surveys are conducted with people who no longer do business with your company. These people will be predominantly the Amiable personality type, who would rather switch than fight. When this survey is being conducted, it should be done by a "fresh face," someone who hasn't possibly offended the customer.

<u>Survey Method</u>: Telephone.

2. Recovery Standards

Here's a saying that may have made it to your hometown—
"The customer is always right."

In my opinion, that's not the case. The customer is *not* always right, but the customer is always the customer. We gain absolutely zero if we get into a pushing contest with the customer. We will discuss in Chapter Six that there are rare times when you should fire your customer. If the customer is upset because we did something we shouldn't have or didn't do something we were supposed to have done, we have to make it right. There is a correlation between a company's financial success and its recovery standards. Pick up the ball quickly after you fumble it, and you will win the game. Drop the ball and leave it lying on the ground, and you will almost inevitably lose, no matter how wonderful your service or product is.

On a business trip to Vancouver I had asked for an early check-in at the downtown hotel where I was to stay. As I approached the desk clerk and reminded her of my prior arrangement, I was met with the cheeriest, brightest smile you could imagine. "Good news, Mr. Morris, your room isn't quite ready!"

My first response was that she was making fun of my situation and that I was within my rights to get angry.

"What that means" she continued, "is that during your stay here, we will pay for all of your breakfasts."

Since the average cost of breakfast at this hotel was in the $16 range, I was okay with the fact my room wasn't ready. Before I left, they had added to their recovery process by placing in my room a souvenir coffee mug, a furry squeegee for my computer monitor screen, along with a handwritten note of apology from my main contact, the sales and catering manager.

Will I stay there again? Of course. The minor inconvenience was more than offset by their effective recovery program.

The key to your successful recovery program is to reply:

Rapidly
Massively

Each industry will have its own recovery program. Your recovery program is really nothing more than an insurance policy. Your customers are being insured, whether they know it or not, against you messing up.

Prism Inc. takes it a step further. Prism's main reason for being is that they eliminate pests from becoming the focal point at restaurants and hotels who retain their services. At Prism, though, they understand that what they are selling, pest control, is not what their customers are buying. In fact their customers are buying an insurance policy against furry, creepy, and/or winged pests disrupting their customers' revenue stream. That's right, their customers are purchasing insurance. Prism's guarantee (recovery program) promises no pests. If pests appear that were not caused by negligence on the part of the hotel or restaurant owner, Prism will not only refund the customer's monthly service fee but will also assume the meal or room charges of the wronged customer and send a note of apology. If the situation reaches extreme proportions and calls for a facility to be closed down by the board of health, Prism will reimburse the customer for the amount of the fine and provide support in dealing with the authorities.[7]

That is a recovery standard that will be tough to beat.

Recovery is the first step in setting Power of WOW! standards. TARP (Technical Assistance Research Program) is a non-profit organization based in Arlington, Virginia, which provides feedback through surveys and studies on customer-service-related topics.

The bar chart on the following page shows the effects of bouncing back after various responses to having the ball dropped.

---

[7] Richard Whitely and Diane Hessan, *Customer Centered Growth,* (Addison-Wesley, Reading, Massachusetts., 1996) page 31.

The Bounce Back Effect
Figure 3.1

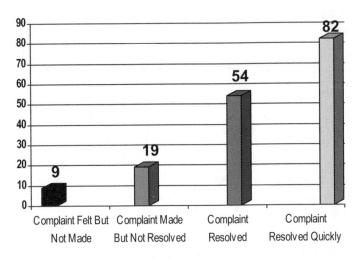

Study done by TARP Institute

   The bar farthest left represents the nine per cent of people who felt a complaint but didn't register it. These people will likely be the Amiable personality style, with a few of the Analytical personality style thrown in for good measure. These folks would rather switch than fight. Studies tell us that for every customer who complains, there are twenty-three others who feel the same complaint but won't verbalize it. It's tough to recover this group because you won't know for a long time that you have ticked them off. They will vote quietly with their wallets or purses and slink off to begin a business relationship with one of your competitors.

   The next bar, second from the left represents people who took the time to lodge a complaint but felt the complaint wasn't solved to their satisfaction. As you can see, it's pretty tough to build a business if you can only recover a quarter of your customers when you upset them.

The next bar shows that fifty-four per cent of people who felt the complaint was resolved to their satisfaction. It's still not great. What do they want, cartwheels? No, but it looks like they do want speed.

The bar on the far right shows that a full eighty-two per cent of people will deal with you again if you fix their problem, and fix it *now!* Too many companies are hesitant to empower their front-line servers to solve the problem. Have you ever had a situation where you have had a problem with a company, only to be told by the front-line server that you will have to wait to speak to their manager, who will be in tomorrow? When the next day comes and the manager doesn't call you, you may be mildly surprised. You will also be mildly surprised to discover that the manager can't solve the problem either but will be glad to refer it to the division manager who will be back from holidays on Monday. When you have to call the division manager (because he or she wouldn't consider calling you) you are no longer mildly surprised. You aren't even surprised to find out that they have to refer it to the regional manager, who should be hired any day now!

This may be a slight exaggeration, but all of us have at some time had a similar experience. Empower your people. Let *them* become the problem-solvers and heroes that they deserve to be.

Ritz Carlton Hotels are customer-service leaders, partially because they have great properties and great service. They also have a great recovery program. Every employee at Ritz Carlton is allotted $2,000 annually to make customer problems go away. This amount can be spent at the discretion of any employee, from chambermaid to CEO. The company found that very few employees ever use the full amount every year, but just having the ability and power to solve a problem makes them confident in dealing with customer complaints. Don't hesitate to empower your front-line staff. They have a much bigger impact on customer satisfaction *and* customer loyalty than an ivory tower V.P. of Something That Will Make Our Customer Happy, who takes more than two days to solve the problem.

3. Image Standards

Have you ever made an appointment to see your doctor and then spent an hour or more in the waiting room? Sometimes this will happen even if you call ahead to see if he's running on time. Is this professional service? We think it must be, because our doctor is a professional. When you're on the receiving end of this treatment, though, the service seems a little shoddy.

Another perceived group of professionals are lawyers. But have you ever dealt with a lawyer, then clutched your chest when you got the bill? You're charged for photocopies, phones calls, staples, and maybe even Twinkies! When you call to question the bill, your phone call is returned when? Approximately? That's right—never! Yet these are people we look up to as professionals.

Wow! Customer Service is about *personal accountability*. You don't have to have a bunch of letters behind your name to be perceived as a professional, but you do have to be accountable to yourself, your team, your process, and, above all, your customers. If you can become accountable in the following twelve areas, you will be perceived as professional.

Twelve Keys to Being Perceived as a Professional

I. **Master/Mistress of Details** – Make sure that the "i"s are dotted and the "t"s are crossed. If paper is a big part of your workaday world, make sure that it's complete, correct, and on time. So often, it's the little things in life that make all the difference, yet the little things are so easy to overlook. One group I facilitated had one young individual who felt that her lack of attention to detail was causing her so much stress in her workplace that she committed to become a Dominatrix of Details. If you have to take it a step further, by all means, take it a step further!

II. **Have the Ability to Anticipate Your Customers' Needs** – You can accomplish this by knowing as much as you can about your customers' business. We are WOW!ed by someone who understands our business, aren't we? Why should our customers be any different from us? Check your customers' Web sites, their annual reports, the phone book, industry publications, or any number of sources you need, to become aware of what their business stresses are. Then, think about how you can make that stress disappear.

III. **Have a "Can-do" Attitude** – As customers, we want to deal with people who say to us "No problem!" or "That's my favorite challenge!" Even if you can't meet a customer's specific request, you don't have to verbalize it. "Here's what I can do!" will indicate that a solution is on the horizon, without ever having to say "No" to a customer.

IV. **Develop Mental Toughness** – Your customers don't care if you just broke up with your significant other, received a "Congratulations, you have just won a revenue audit from the government" letter, totaled you car, or have the hangover from hell. To your customers, only their problems are real, only their situations are worth discussing. They are correct. They expect you to be as sharp and accommodating at 6:00 p.m., Friday, as you were at 10:00 a.m., Monday, no matter what has happened in between.

V. **Be Consistent at Generating Results** – No matter our company or our position, at the end of the day, we are paid for one thing, the results we generate. It's easy to be seduced into filling our days with tasks we enjoy and are good at. If we can't perform our responsibilities with any degree of consistency, though, we may be viewed as less than professional by customers, co-workers, and employers.

VI. **Develop Extensive Product Knowledge** – To be truly perceived as a professional, go the extra mile on this one. Learn about not just your own products but your competitors' products as well. Learn also the reasons that people buy your goods and services. They are not, in their mind, buying what you sell. Instead, they are buying *solutions to their problems*. As the old saying goes: "People don't buy the drill, they buy the half-inch hole." Be the first one on your block to get in tune to the fact that your customers aren't buying your widgets, they are instead buying peace of mind, image, safety, security, or some other intangible. Still, that knowledge starts with you knowing your product, and the problems that it causes to disappear in a puff of smoke.

VII. **Be a Person of Integrity** – To me, integrity has two major components, honesty and reliability. Be the kind of person that can be counted on to do what is right for the customer, even if it may cost your company some business in the short term. Reliability calls on you only to do what you said you were going to do, and how tough is that? Do it right. Do it right the first time. Do it right the first time on time. Do this, and you will already be better than most companies on the street.

VIII. **Become Passionate about Making a Difference** – If you set out at the beginning of the day to help as many people as you can, instead of trying to sell as much as you can, you will have a rewarding career, and you will be looked upon as someone who makes a difference. Zig Ziglar says, "Help people get what they want, and you will get everything that you want."

IX. **Dedicate Yourself to Personal Excellence** – It is in our own best interest to become as valuable as we can. We have to remember that we aren't being paid for the hour. If that was the case we could phone our employer at the end of the week from home and say, "Pay me for forty hours, please." That would be too easy. Instead, we are paid for the *value* that we bring to the hour. The best way to increase our value is to choose a path that will see us improve as employees, as employers, as teammates, as husbands, and wives. I once read that you should invest seven-and-a-half per cent of your net income and seven-and-a-half per cent of your working time to becoming personally excellent. That is to say, if you net $40,000 a year, you should be investing $3,000 on courses, seminars, and books, as well as audio and video programs. If you work 200 days a year, then fifteen days should be devoted to making yourself more valuable.

> *"Formal education will make you a living.*
> *Self-education will make you a fortune."*
>
> Jim Rohn

I always get a little down when I run into recent university graduates at my seminars who tell me,

79

"I'm just here because I have to be here. I promised myself I wouldn't crack another book on learning as long as I live. I've had enough of that." That's great. They are twenty-one years old, and they're as good as they're going to get.

X. **Be Respectful** – Learn to respect the differences between customers. Some are wise and some are not. Some are polite and some are not. Some have integrity and some do not. Some are in a hurry and some are not. They all have one thing in common, though. They deserve our respect. It is especially important that we respect their time.

XI. **Become Known for Your Image** – Image is about how you walk, how you talk, how you appear to others, and how you conduct yourself. Are you a positive person or are you known in business circles as a whiner? Is your dress appropriate for your job? How about your language? Image can have a huge impact on whether or not you are perceived as a professional.

XII. **Develop a Strong Work Ethic** – Maybe this should have been number one, because without this ingredient the others don't much matter. Become used to doing more on the job than is expected of you. To some of you, this sounds plain silly. For others already living it, you will recognize it as an investment in you future.

Ask yourself, "Which one of these qualities am I going to improve on over the next twenty-one days to make myself more professional?" Write your answer down on a piece of paper and put it where you will see it every day for the next twenty-one days. There may be more than one you would like to improve on, but make sure you pick one category so you can focus on that area only for the next three-week period. Since it takes twenty-one days to develop a new habit, you should have made enough progress after that period to move on to another area that you may think needs improvement. Don't work on more than one at a time, it just doesn't work.

4. Client Communication Standards

As we will see, not every person responds well to the same treatment. The chances are that these differences come down to "Working Styles." Working Styles is a term coined by Dr. David Merrill of Tracom Consulting Group. In our seminars, we call these Personality Styles, but let's give Dr. Merrill his due. Learning to recognize and work with the different Personality Styles is priceless.

Dr. Merrill set out to measure two things in human beings: Responsiveness and Assertiveness.

Responsiveness:
He considered the tempo at which people moved physically. Did they move slowly or with rapid strides? Were their movements wild, with frenzied gesticulations, or were they much more understated, with not much latitude? Quiet and withdrawn, or bubbly and outgoing? Were they more apt to want to see, rather than be seen?

Assertiveness:
Next, Dr. Merrill looked how likely individuals would be to impose their will on someone else. Were the individuals determined to have their own way or would they be willing to bend? Did the test subjects speak using forceful language or was their speech soft and encouraging? Were they bent on having their opinions heard, or were they content listening to the opinions of others?

Once Dr. Merrill's studies were complete, he developed a matrix and applied four names to the four different types of people: amiable, expressive, analytical, and driver.

We will see in Chapter Five that what we learn to apply to our external customers is equally important in dealing with our customer-service teams. To fully understand how to get the full benefit from the use of Personality Styles, let's first understand the difference between the Golden Rule and the Platinum Rule.

The Golden Rule:

Do unto others as you would be done unto.

That is a powerful rule to be sure, but what if the person being 'done unto' isn't the least bit like you? What if you are quiet and withdrawn, and the person you are 'doing unto' is loud and brassy? Isn't there a good chance that they don't understand where you are coming from? When this happens, instead of feeling they are 'being done unto,' they simply feel they are 'being done.' Instead of the Golden Rule, where we put our values on others, let's apply the Platinum Rule, which features only a subtle difference.

The Platinum Rule:

Treat others as they would like to be treated.

Doesn't that make more sense, to treat people as *they* would like, rather than as *we* would like? How often has a new customer been introduced to your business, who is *so* sympathetic that you can almost finish their sentences for them?! A short time later, another person introduced to your business is so obtuse, you find yourself asking, "What planet is this loser from?"

Those in the first group may or may not be great people, but they likely have the same Personality Style as you. Thus, their values, their points of reference, the things that they think are either funny or tragic, are likely similar to yours. You don't have to take a course or even read any further to begin to understand these people. Unfortunately, there are billions of people out there who fit into the second group who are not like you, so read on and at least understand why they say and do the things they do.

Personality Style Quadrants
Figure 3.2

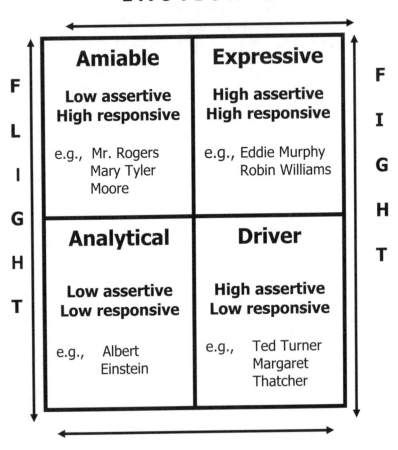

AMIABLE

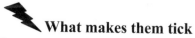

What makes them tick

They are very much into *relationships*, and have a strong need for *acceptance*. These people are *non-confrontational* and would rather switch their attitudes, opinions, and choices than fight. Statistics tell us that only four per cent of complaints are verbalized. You can bet that the remaining ninety-six per cent of people are, in large part, made up of the amiable personality type. When they play the part of an external customer, they are both good-news and bad-news bears. The good news is that they don't complain when they feel they have been wronged. The bad news is that they don't come back. The even worse news is that they will tell their friends. The worst news is they have a lot of friends!

Characteristics

Some characteristics of Amiables are a tendency to show a low degree of assertiveness, but a high degree of responsiveness. As clients, they want to be your friend, and they want you to be theirs. They will do business with the person they like the most and trust the most. If purchasing your product or service will make them stand out in a crowd, or have the least potential to cause conflict or disruption in their lives, you will have a hard time selling to them.

Other words that describe the amiable personality style would be:

⌘ **Tolerant**
⌘ **Cooperative**
⌘ **Friendly**
⌘ **Polite**
⌘ **Sociable**
⌘ **Supportive**
⌘ **Patient**

Phrases that will motivate an Amiable

"Let's solve this problem together."

"Can I give you my opinion?"

"How do you *feel* about it?"

"Tell me about your family."

Amiables are not so good at making decisions. They can slow a purchase by making sure the decision is okay with everyone. They will want to shop at least in pairs, with their spouse, significant other, or a close friend. Be patient, be low-key, be friendly, and never even think about pressuring them into buying your product or service.

EXPRESSIVE

 What makes them tick

These folks are *fun* to be with. In fact that is one of their greatest traits. *They have little fear of risk* and will happily tread where angels fear to go. They have an *aversion to detail* and may offer *strong opinions.*

What really drives an expressive though, is *image.* They may want to make a fashion statement. Their clothes will be a little more flamboyant than most people's, and if they are in the world of business, they will appear very crisp. They will have expensive dry-cleaning bills. While they are willing to take risks with an unproven product, and they want a lot of fun in their business dealings, image is the biggest motivator for these folks. They want the newest, the brightest, the biggest, the whizziest, or the best. If you can combine all of these things, all the better!

 Characteristics

Expressive people show a high degree of assertiveness as well as a high degree of responsiveness. They love being the center of attention and will sometimes do outlandish things to draw attention to themselves. Acknowledge that side of them. If it's not too far out of your comfort zone, join in the fun. A great example of an Expressive would be actor Robin Williams.

Other words that describe the expressive personality would be:

⌘ **Outgoing**
⌘ **Gregarious**
⌘ **Popular**
⌘ **Showy**
⌘ **Dramatic**
⌘ **Humorous**

Phrases that will motivate an Expressive
"You'll be the first one on you block to have this."
"This will make you look really good!"
"This product is lots of fun!"
"This will give you access to well-known people."
     One shortcoming of Expressives is that they may seem shallow to the other working styles. Their greatest strength, their ability to have fun and be the center of attention, can seem to be overdone by some. The less assertive personality styles, like Amiables and especially Analyicals, have to have patience when presenting their product or service, because the Expressive's desire to do business is *all* about them. Don't feel put out or offended when the Expressive has a laugh at the expense of your offering. At least grin and bear it, and, as mentioned above, if it's in you, join in the fun.

ANALYTICAL

What makes them tick

For the most part, Analyticals are more motivated by technical terminology, mechanical equipment, and numerical values than they are by people. Their key hot buttons are *fact, data, and information*. They also have a *desire to be correct*. For this reason, never bet with an Analytical, because you can be sure they have researched the information and are likely correct

Characteristics

Analyticals have a low degree of assertiveness as well as a low degree of responsiveness. They are driven by information and they have an overwhelming desire to be correct. Don't be surprised if they know more about the technical aspects of your product than you do. They also come from Missouri, the Show Me State. Don't make exaggerated claims about your offering. No matter that you state your product is the greatest thing since sliced bread, until it's proven to an Analytical, they still think that sliced bread is pretty good. You won't want to be overly flamboyant in your presentation. Be factual, be concise, and don't be too personal.

Other words that may describe analytical personality may be:

⌘ Somber
⌘ Factual
⌘ Thinking
⌘ Serious
⌘ Reserved
⌘ Logical
⌘ Systematic

Phrases that will motivate an Analytical

"Here are the pros and cons."

"Can I make an appointment to see you?"

"This product is reliable based on the following statistics as presented in the *Harvard Business Review*."

DRIVER

 What makes them tick

These people are most motivated by getting things done. They are intense, achieving people. They are most concerned with the *bottom line* and r*esults*. They must have *control* in any interaction. They might also offer their *opinion*. They have an opinion, usually a strong opinion, on just about everything. They will tell you their opinion, and if they want to know yours, they'll tell you what that is, too!

Characteristics

Drivers can be recognized as having low emotional responsiveness but high levels of assertiveness. If they are walking, they are in a hurry. If they are talking, they want to be heard. If they are sitting at a computer keyboard, their fingers are flying. These folks are so intense that they will build a garage in the morning, try to find a cure for cancer in the afternoon, and have a full evening of skiing! They may be viewed as being rude and abrupt. They don't suffer fools lightly. A good example of a Driver would be General Norman Schwarzkopf of Desert Storm fame, or George Steinbrenner of the New York Yankees.

When Dealing with these people, respect their time. Be punctual for appointments, and when making presentations, be strong, confident, and credible. Even if you have the best solution to their problem or concern, it's imperative that you give them a couple of options. It's about control. They get to pick, not you.

Other words that would accurately describe a Driver would be:

- ⌘ **Decisive**
- ⌘ **Autonomous**
- ⌘ **Deliberate**
- ⌘ **Impatient**
- ⌘ **Focused**
- ⌘ **Opinionated**

 Phrases that will motivate a Driver

"This won't take long."

"This will save you money because . . ."

"This will save you time by . . ."

A Word of Caution

The real power in using the Personality Styles is that it helps you to first understand, rather than be understood. Once you become conversant with this information, you may feel the urge to use it for personal gain. Repress that urge! This information is about understanding, not manipulation. There will come a time that you become so very adept at using the Personality Styles that you may not see the harm in using 'smoke and mirrors' on a customer to make a sale, or to up-sell a product or service. Do so at your own peril. Besides being unethical, it introduces the potential of shattering your customer's trust, leaving you with a reputation as a manipulative character. That is infinitely more costly than losing a customer.

Different Personality Styles as Customers

Unless you know differently, you will tend to treat every customer in the same manner. Since we all have different personality styles, sometimes this will work, and sometimes it won't. Here are a few examples of the wrong and right way to handle interactions with different Personality Styles.

Wrong

Let's assume that Dick Driver wants a winter vacation in Cancun, and he heads to the nearest travel agency where he encounters Anna-Marie Amiable. This is what would normally transpire:

Dick Driver: *I want your best price for two weeks in Cancun.*

Anna-Marie Amiable: *Oh, you'll absolutely love Cancun this time of year! I was there about a year ago, and the people were so friendly. It has beaches to die for, and...*

Dick Driver (interrupting): *So what's your best price?*

Anna-Marie Amiable (gushing): *Well, there are so many great deals. We have all-inclusive for two weeks at the Gran Caribe, or the Hyatt Cancun resort, which are wonderful properties, but a little pricey. The Casa Maya is also very pretty, but not so ...*

Dick Driver (getting miffed): *Look, I'm pressed for time, so could you tell me the best ...*

Anna-Marie Amiable (bordering on euphoria): *And if golf is your thing, well, the golf course on the lagoon is...*

Dick Driver (now totally incensed): *What a jerkwater outfit! I'm going to where I can get a simple answer to a simple question, you simple person!*

Anna-Marie Amiable (bursting into tears): *What did I say? I was only trying to help.*

Right

What would have made this interaction more pleasant for both parties? Anna-Marie should have recognized Dick as a Driver from the outset. His opening question was short and to the point. He also posed a bottom-line question. Rather than gushing and giving Dick more detail than he needed, a better approach would have been the following:

91

Dick Driver: *I want your best price to Cancun.*

Anna-Marie Amiable: *Certainly. Right now I my best price for one week is an all-inclusive at the Casa Maya for $1,595, or two weeks all-inclusive at the Gran Caribe for $2,295. Do either of these sound appealing?*

Dick Driver: *I only have a week to spare. Is the Casa Maya a good place?*

Anna-Marie Amiable: *It's the best value for the dollar.*

Dick Driver: *Sounds like it's for me.*

The difference in the two scenarios is that Anna-Marie recognized immediately that Dick, as a Driver, wasn't there to visit. He wanted the bottom line, pronto, and Anna-Marie complied. She also recognized that, as a Driver, Dick needed control. She gave him options, and he picked the one that suited him best. She also didn't supply him with a lot of detail. Had he wanted more, he would have asked. Anna-Marie, being relationship oriented, may have felt a little out of her comfort zone, but she did what was the best for her customer.

Let's try a similar scenario, where Edie Expressive goes to the same travel agency, where she encounters Analytical Al:

Wrong

Edie Expressive (flouncing her hair): *G'day, Mate! Tell me all about Australia, Dude! I can't wait to sample surf, Fosters, some of that prime Aussie beefcake! What can you tell me?*

Analytical Al: *What do you mean, 'Aussie beefcake'? In fact Australia is better known for sheep.*

Edie Expressive: *You know, Dude—rugby players, surfers, crocodile wrestlers. The handsome body beautiful from Down Under! What can you tell me?*

Analytical Al: *To begin with, my name isn't 'Dude'; it's Al. I have a complete list of packages, tours, prices, references, locations, and a variety of options to choose from, from bed and breakfasts to all-inclusive to out back tours. Here is one tour in particular that I find interesting. It's called 'Fascinating Walking Tours of Sydney's Libraries.' I have a detailed brochure on the subject if you are ...*

  Edie Expressive: *Sheesh! What a wet blanket!*
  Analytical Al: *What do you mean by that?*

Right
This interaction would have been made more enjoyable from the outset had Al recognized Edie's Personality Style as Expressive. The verbal clues she gave, being very familiar and obviously interested in the fun aspects of travel were likely only part of the story. In real life, Edie probably gave some visual clues as well. As an Expressive she may have been wearing something that made a fashion statement. Al's next mistake was being literal and making an issue of the 'beefcake' comment. As an Analytical, Al didn't want Edie to get away without being aware that sheep were a big deal in Australia. He had to assert his knowledge. He was on the edge of bogging her down with detail. This example may seem extreme, but I have seen similar scenes played out in front of me on numerous occasions. Here's what would have been better:

  Edie the Expressive (flouncing her hair): *G'day, Mate! Tell me all about Australia, Dude! I can't wait to sample some of that surf, Fosters, and prime Australian beefcake! What can you tell me?*

  Al the Analytical: *G'day to you! If it's fun you're after, a very popular spot has been Surfer's Paradise on Australia's Gold Coast. The Mark and the Olympus are noted action night hotspots, and some of the best restaurants and shopping in the world are within a few bocks of the beach. Does that sound like what you're looking for, dudette?*

Edie the Expressive: *Does that sound like it? Wow! It sounds like paradise!*

Al the Analytical: *Precisely.*

Al saw right off that Edie displayed the traits of an Expressive by her off-the-wall greeting, and he got in on track with her immediately with his snappy comeback. It was obvious that Edie just wanted to have fun, so without too much detail, Al pointed out an area that positively wreaks of good times. Al stepped out of his comfort zone by saying that the best facilities in the world were at hand. In recognizing Edie as an Expressive, he didn't have to go into detail for her to accept that good times were at hand. Edie was looking to buy fun and image. In this scenario, that's what Al happened to be selling. Both parties win.

Let's play that again, this time with the roles reversed.

Wrong

Analytical Al: *Good morning. I was contemplating a trip to Africa, and I was wondering what information ...*

Edie the Expressive (jumping in with both feet): *Ah, Africa! The Dark Continent. Don't you think they should invest in some lights? Ha, ha! It's supposed to be fun. There are some good beaches somewhere on the West coast, and I think some on the other coast as well. What will it be, west or other?*

Analytical Al (pondering): *I was actually more interested in some of the historical sites of ...*

Edie the Expressive: *History? Who cares? That's a long way to go for history! If you want my opinion ...*

Analytical Al: *I don't, thank you. Could you supply me with a detailed list of the other travel agents in this area, though?*

In this case, Edie was too quick to put her values and opinions on Al. In fairness to Edie, Al never had a lot of opportunity to demonstrate his personality style, although it was clear it wasn't the same as Edie's. She was intent on making a joke, staying the focus of attention, and sharing her opinion. Had she listened more intently, she wouldn't have pressed Al for a decision before he had all the facts.

Right

This would have been a more effective meeting had Edie listened to Al. The verbal hints he was about to give should have given her enough information to do what was right for Al. This scenario would have played out better.

Analytical Al: *Good morning. I was contemplating a trip to Africa, and I was wondering if you have any information on the origins of the slave trade. I find it an interesting topic.*

Edie the Expressive: *I would be more than willing to share what we have. May I ask why you have an interest?*

Analytical Al: *Yes. I teach world history at the university, and to date I have been able to visit two other continents. I like to get as much detail as I can on each subject and each time frame. On my wall in my office I have a chart that demonstrates what was happening in different parts of the world in the same era. My expertise on events in Africa is somewhat limited. I want to experience Africa first-hand.*

Edie the Expressive: *It's always nice to meet an expert. We don't get a lot of call for exactly what you are looking for, but I do have some information on tours in Ghana, West Africa. There is a guided tour of the prison at Cape Coast, where prisoners were held before being sent to Europe and North America from the 1600s to the 1800s. You actually get to go to the dungeons. The man that runs the company has been in business for twenty-five years, and he offers a 'safety guarantee' with his tours. There are a number of brochures on other tours in the area, including a safari at Mole National Park, not far away. This tour is run by the same company that runs the Cape Coast tour, and the same guarantee applies.*

Analytical Al: *That sounds interesting.*

Edie the Expressive: *If I could make a suggestion, why don't you take these brochures and examine them at your leisure. Get back to me at your convenience. There is one more thing you may find helpful, though. The Africa On-line Web site has current information on what is going on in all regions of Africa. You may want to check that out.*

Analytical Al: *You have been most helpful. I will be back once I analyze the data. You may not believe it, but the last travel agent I talked to tried to send me to a beach!*

Edie the Expressive: *Go figure.*

By listening, Edie was able to determine Al's Personality Style and his needs. The fact that a chart was his first choice of wall décor was a massive clue. She was right to acknowledge his expert status and to give him time to make a decision. She also supplied him with as much data as she possibly could. In the real world, Al would have to take a lot of time to analyze the data, but since Edie is just like him, he will be back.

Let's wrap this up with Anna-Marie and Dick again. The reason that I have chosen these particular pairings is because Amiables/Drivers and Expressives/Analyticals are positioned diagonally on the matrix. They are as close to opposite as you will find. If one of these pairs can get on track with the other, it is a testament to understanding. That's what this information allows us to do. We will be able to understand people whose point of reference is totally different from ours so well that we will have an uncanny ability to relate to them and make doing business a pleasurable experience for both parties. But back to Dick and Anna-Marie.

Wrong

Anna-Marie Amiable (positively bouncy): *A great good morning to you, sir! I have two weeks' vacation coming, and a couple of friends and I are planning a holiday to where the sand beaches are warm and the people are friendly. I am just gathering information right now, but what would you recommend? Of course, I will need their approval.*

Dick Driver: *Cancun's good.*

Anna-Marie Amiable: *Oh, I'm sure it is, or you wouldn't have said that! What about the people? Are they friendly? Is it easy to meet people on day tours? My friend, Analytical Al, was saying just the other day that ...*

Dick Driver: *I said it was good. Good value. Fair prices.*

Anna-Marie Amiable: *What is the night life like? I heard that it has the biggest night club in the world. I'll bet that place is packed at night. We could meet dozens of people there, couldn't we?*

Dick Driver: *Look, lady, you can do what you want. Are you here to buy or just visit? I have things to do.*

Anna-Marie Amiable: *Well, I am sorry to be a bother. Is it all right if I go to another travel agency for information?*

Dick Driver: *Be my guest.*

Right

Dick would have had more success with Anna Marie had he been able to get on the personal side of the relationship. She gave ample clues, asking about how to meet people, the night life that everyone must experience there, and informing Dick up front that she still needed her group's approval. Why, she was amiable to the end, when she asked Dick's permission to take here business elsewhere. Dick on the other hand was a true Driver, being gruff, answering in short bursts, and concerned only with the bottom line. He could care less to see her walk, since he had pre-determined that his bottom line wasn't going to be affected in the short term.

This would have had a happier ending had Dick cared enough to live both for the present and the future. In the previous scenario Anna-Marie would have sensed conflict, and would never have returned. Let's see what Dick could have done just a little bit differently.

Anna-Marie Amiable: *A great good morning to you, sir! I have two weeks' vacation coming, and a couple of friends and I are planning a holiday to where the sand beaches are warm and the people are friendly. I'm gathering information now, but what would you recommend? Of course I will need their approval.*

Dick Driver: *Cancun is very popular this time of year.*

Anna-Marie Amiable: *Oh, I'm sure it is, or you wouldn't have said that! What about the people? Are they friendly? Is it easy to meet people on day tours? My friend, Analytical Al, was saying just the other day that ...*

Dick Driver: *Do you know Analytical Al? I know him, too. He's a great guy, isn't he?*

Anna-Marie Amiable: *Oh, he sure is. We were really looking forward to going to some clubs where everybody goes.*

Dick Driver: *Well, then, Cancun is for you. The biggest nightclub in the world is there, and it's supposed to be packed from sundown to sunup. Say, do you mind if I make a suggestion?*

Anna-Marie Amiable: *By all means!*

Dick Driver: *Why don't you bring Al here, and we can go through the necessary information as a group. It would be nice to see him again. Is there anyone else who you would have to speak with in order to make a decision?*

Anna-Marie Amiable: *Well, yes. Edie the Expressive is the life of the party, and she'll be coming.*

Dick Driver: *Why not bring her along, too. It sounds like she would be a good person to get to know.*

Anna-Marie Amiable: *That sounds like a great idea. When should we come by?*

Dick Driver: *Is Saturday morning a good time? I'll have the coffee on.*

Anna-Marie Amiable: *It sounds marvelous. I am so looking forward to the four of us getting together.*

Dick Driver: *Me too!*

Dick was able to win Anna-Marie over without taking a huge step out of his comfort zone. While he wasn't overly verbose, he conveyed early on that Anna-Marie's chosen destination was popular, which is a must for the Amiable working style. Without a lot of effort he was able to turn the shopping trip into a group activity, which also appealed to Anna-Marie. He asked permission to give his opinion. Without taking on Anna-Marie's characteristics, he was able to turn the interaction into potential business for his company, and Anna-Marie was delighted to meet a new friend.

Standards are like fire. They can be the most useful tool imaginable, but they can burn you like nothing else if you let them get away on you. Standards apply to everyone in the organization, from the rank and file on up to the top executive. They will only be effective though if they flow from the top down. Standards must be demonstrated and adopted by the uppermost echelon. Too often a company will spend a fortune in cash, time, and energy on developing standards for the rank and file. These standards will have no staying power, though, if they are not embraced by upper management. In fact nothing will deep-six an initiative faster than having upper management say one thing and do another. Standards will not survive hypocrisy. The company's top brass must develop the mantra "Do as I say *and* as I do." Living the company's culture works from the top down.

SECTION III

EXECUTING

THE

PLAN

Chapter Four

From the Top Down

> *"As we are impressed, so we express."*
>
> Aristotle

Leaders from great companies have taken a page from Aristotle's book. They know that the way they lead their companies will be emulated by their staff, from their executive team, through the middle ranks, and right on down to the front-line server, and all of those people who support the team but do not directly touch the customer. If the staff observe the leader treating the customer as the most important person on earth, the staff will follow. If the staff observe the leader speaking convincingly of his wonderful product, service, and teams, the staff will follow suit. So if the leader speaks contemptuously of or to customers, the message is that it's permissible for everyone in the organization to act in a like manner. If the leader is seen pointing fingers, assessing blame on others, and denying blame himself, staff will respond in kind when placed in the same situation. The question usually asked in these companies is not "Where do we go from here?" but rather "Whose fault was this screw-up?"

If, however, the leader is committed to personally executing the high standards of the company, the staff, too, will make the same commitment. This comes back to the culture that the leader has instilled in the company.

Lessons in Customer Service

Power of WOW! companies and their CEOs realize the sizable role that corporate culture plays in employee and customer loyalty. There are any number of critical factors to consider when starting a company, but the most important may be corporate culture. It is the secret ingredient that has the capacity to separate visionary companies from those that flounder. One of the most challenging tasks you will face as a leader is how to instill your vision and values in your team so that you are able to extract the most positive skills and attitudes from each of them. As important as this is, research demonstrates that most managers and team leaders are woefully inadequate at assisting members of their team to reach their full potential. Lominger Limited Inc., a Minnesota-based research firm, determined that of the key sixty-seven leadership competencies that they follow, the importance of "understanding people" ranked in the top ten. The same study showed that North American managers rated dead last, sixty-seventh out of sixty-seven in this essential category.

What are the differentiating factors between companies with a WOW! Customer Service culture and companies with inferior cultures? My opinion is that they realize, first and foremost, that customers do not conduct business with companies. Customers are people who do business with other people, just like themselves. In fact, customers don't even see themselves solely as customers. They see themselves as people first, who happen to be customers. The more you can inspire your team members to appreciate and care for the people that are your customers, the sooner you will develop a powerful customer-service culture. Of the companies that I have studied or experienced first-hand, the companies that have a recognized WOW! Customer Service culture have at least this in common:

1.   The leaders of the culture recognize the value of people, both internally and externally.

2.   These leaders clearly demonstrate the ability to instill their personal values in their individual team members.

3.   They lead by example. They recognize that your team won't buy into your cultures even minimally, if you, as leader, say one thing, then do the opposite.

4. They recognize and appreciate the strengths that different personalities contribute to the good of the corporation.

Companies such as Westjet have unashamedly given the same credence to corporate culture that Southwest Airlines does, whose business model Westjet copied. "It's focus number one. Our risk, in my view, is internal, not external, and that's why we put so much emphasis on it," states Westjet president and CEO Clive Beddoe.

While a strong corporate culture is more visible in large companies, you don't have to be part of a huge corporation to have a winning culture. I found this out first-hand when I was dealing with one of Western Canada's leading businesses, Prairie Meats. "If you don't believe in something, you won't stand up for anything."

So says Gene Dupuis, the company's president. The company has grown from a staff of five in 1983 to around sixty employees today. The company has grown steadily, in no small part due to the commitment of Gene and his partner and brother, Louis, and their ability to build and meld a cohesive customer-service team. During a meeting with Gene I was able to gain insights on the importance of being a leader that instills his values in his team.

1. Hire for attitude, train for skill

When the company started, Gene, the front man for the operation, and now salesguy extraordinaire, was a meat cutter. One of his first potential hires was a meat cutter. Gene stated, "He couldn't cut meat worth a darn. But he had a spark, something in his attitude that I liked." In his not-so-subtle way Gene told his potential new hire, "I don't know how to say this but to say it. I think you'd be a good fit for our new company, but you don't know how to cut meat. Go with Louis, and he will show you how to cut meat to make money."

At the time, premium wages were an issue for the fledgling company, so Gene sold his man on quality of life.

The butcher, previously employed by a large food chain, had to work any hours his employer was open. "Come with us," Gene said, "and you won't have to work a Sunday or an evening shift again." Today, that meat cutter, Tim Grabowski is a valued and valuable employee. He is one of the company's longest-serving employees, and now oversees departments. Dupuis points to another of his 'generals,' Bernie Nowoselski, as being the same type of person as Grabowski. Like the Dupuis brothers, she came from a rural background and had a strong work ethic but limited training. "Her attitude was to do whatever it takes to get the job done" Dupuis stated. "You can't teach that." Perhaps Dupuis recognized a little of himself in his top employees. Gene quit school at age seventeen to join his brother, Louis, in Edmonton. The firm that hired him to his first meat-cutting job hired fifty-seven individuals to the same position that same day. Ten days later, only Gene Dupuis remained. He credits that to a strong work ethic forged in rural roots, and a loving family. He and Louis run their business with a family atmosphere to this day. Another attitude that prevails is that of respect. "There are two hallmarks that we live by. First, we respect effort. Secondly, we respect others. All of the people that have moved to the top of our company have these traits. They are team players, and get to the top through their own actions, not by stepping on others." While each one required training in his or her original field, each one displayed an attitude that fit with the company's winning culture.

2. Lead by example

One of Prairie Meats's radio commercials states, " We don't train our staff to be friendly, we hire friendly people to be our staff." True to its advertising, a spirit of camaraderie and fun is prevalent when you shop there. Counter people kibitz with co-workers and customers alike. It feels like a good place to shop.

Recently, I was asked to facilitate a customer-service workshop for the company, an evening session, which was strictly voluntary. Well over half of the staff showed up, and the participation was excellent. How is it that companies that don't need the training always invest in it? Could there be a message here?

A point that wasn't missed by the staff was that senior management and owners attended and participated on the same level as the front-line and production people. Far too often, company leaders call and say, "Our customer service stinks. Come and fix it." When training day comes, the person who called is nowhere to be found, but probably spending time with his or her family, or shopping, or doing any number of things that the staff isn't being forced to miss.

Herb Kelleher, who has been either CEO or president of Southwest Airlines since its inception in 1967 is another person who understands the power of leading by example. Every Thanksgiving, Kelleher heads down to Love Field, Southwest's home base, and helps to load planes. That is why you aren't surprised to see Southwest pilots picking up garbage in effort to help the cabin staff ensure that Southwest's patented rapid turnaround time is met. Egos are checked at the door, and everyone follows the example of the leader.

3. Make your values known, then live them

As with any number of businesses, the best day of the week for retail meat sales is Saturday. Every seven years, Remembrance Day, November 11th, falls on a Saturday. While more and more businesses chose to open on a day meant to honor the veterans of wars, both living and dead, Prairie Meats is an anomaly. "My father spent five years in a hospital following the war," Gene states. "On Remembrance Day, I attend a service. It's something I believe very strongly in." The same goes for Sundays. Their largest competitors are open seven days a week, and remain open until 9:00 p.m., six nights a week. The staff at Prairie Meats have evenings and Sundays with their families. "We have to keep our priorities straight." In fact, a professionally done sign proudly states on the store's entrance door, "Always closed Sundays. Cooking up Family Values." When queried about the impact of Sunday closing on the bottom line, Dupuis is candid: "Do we lose some business? Absolutely. Do we retain quality staff? Absolutely."

Another company that makes their values known is Cover-All Building Systems Inc. The company is one of the fifty best privately run companies in the country. There is no mistaking the importance of promoting the culture and the company's values. Individual signs displaying the company's six principles are prominently displayed throughout production areas, administration offices, lunch rooms, and board rooms. There is no doubt as to what guides the company. The principles are much more than just words. Corporate Community Development Manager Jay Fuller ensures that the culture is promoted by every division. Often with production facilities, an "us"-versus-"them" attitude is pervasive. Fuller tours the plant on a regular basis, promoting the principles, and seeing to it that every production worker understands the magnitude of his contribution to the company. He also knows every employee by name. The following principles are the guiding light of one of Canada's top exporters.

Principle #1 – Maintain honesty and integrity in all aspects of business.
Principle #2 – Genuinely invest in people.
Principle #3 – Cultivate and maintain a culture that enables people to reach their potential.
Principle #4 – Ensure a quality product which dynamically reflects our creativity and ingenuity.
Principle #5 – Develop enthusiastically satisfied customers.
Principle #6 – Recognize that profitability is essential to our ability to achieve our purpose long-term.

The company promotes a bi-weekly stand-up meeting, where employees come together in a spirit of community to discuss not just business but personal accomplishments outside the scope of work and to share in births, deaths, and weddings.

Southwest Airlines understand the power of living your values. They are famous for their exemplary treatment of staff, and by extension each other. A pilot who had applied for a job at Southwest was invited to spend some time with his would-be employers. The Southwest managers admired the man's credentials, which were impeccable. What led to his non-hiring though was his attitude towards others. His condescending manner was not the proper fit for Southwest, where employees are expected to laugh at themselves from time to time.[8]

4. Surround yourself with great people

While the Dupuis brothers lead a WOW! Customer Service company, they admittedly don't have all the answers. "We don't pretend to know everything. My brother, Louis, and I have hired people that know more about certain aspects of the business than we do. The better our people are, the better our company is. The whole is stronger than the sum of its individual parts."

Personal growth is an expectation at Prairie Meats. "Assume the responsibility before it is given," says Dupuis, "and you will thrive in our culture."

---

[8] K. and J. Freiberg, *Nuts!* (Bard Press, Austin, Texas, 1996) page 68.

> *"Hire people smaller than you and you will have a company of dwarfs.*
> *Hire people bigger than you and you will have a company of giants."*
>
> David Ogilvy

View Training as an Investment, not an Expense

Business philosopher Jim Rohn said, "Work harder on yourself than you do on your job." Too many organizations agree with this philosophy, as long as the employee concentrates on that improvement on their own time. This is not the best approach. WOW! Customer Service organizations recognize the need for constant improvement in their people. General Motors' Saturn division is a prime example. They set a training goal of ninety-two hours per year, per employee. Recently, I became a member of the Saturn family. The entire purchase process was a WOW! experience. It started with a polite knowledgeable young salesperson walking me and my wife through a series of well-thought-out questions that uncovered our needs. My two previous vehicles were from an import dealership, and I was a heartbeat away from another purchase from the same dealership. I decided to look elsewhere after the import dealer's salesperson's questioning concluded. He asked:

    1)   "What kind d'ya want?"
    2)   "Wudda ya wanna spend?"

    Not exactly an in-depth sales diagnosis. His lazy attitude conveyed that since he had a good product to sell, he didn't have to work for the sale. Someone should have told him that Customer Service is about people, not things. This guy did any number of things to sabotage his sale—the third time my wife and I went to see him, he couldn't really remember who we were. This was in the span of two weeks. When I asked for a ballpark figure for my trade-in, the same brand that he was selling, he presented me with what I thought was a ridiculously low figure. My reaction must have showed on my face, because he asked immediately what I thought would be a fair price. When I gave him my figure, he actually laughed out loud. He reminded me that my car was more than a few years old. I reminded him that he had just finished telling me what great quality his brand offered, and how well the cars held their value. He reminded me that not only was my car a few years old but it also had high mileage. He won this battle. He was right. Before we got to the next round of negotiations, where I expected he would insult my grandmother and possibly her choice of footwear, I decided to leave with what little dignity I had remaining, protesting wife in tow. My inclination was to sell the car privately and return with cash in hand.

In the end, we sold the car privately for substantially more than the figure the salesman suggested. We advertised a price that we thought was accurate and fair, and the car sold on the first phone call, which came at 7:00 a.m., about the time the newspaper was delivered to most houses. We had over fifty phone calls, and one caller offered to buy the car, sight unseen, for a thousand dollars more than advertised. My first thought was, "I sure missed the boat on that one. I could have put an extra fifteen hundred dollars in my pocket." My second thought was, "That salesman really wanted to take me for a ride—and not a test drive, either!" At this point, it became obvious that a most important ingredient was missing in my relationship with the import salesperson—trust.

Our Saturn sales process followed with an in-depth comparison between the car we were interested in and comparable vehicles that competitors carried. When I defended my car's strengths, my salesman agreed wholeheartedly. He had been trained to realize he wasn't going to gain points by knocking the competition and, by extension, my intelligence.

He then took us on a test drive with him in control of the car to start. As he drove, he explained some of the vehicle's features and benefits. I'm normally not taken with feature and benefit selling, but this guy had earned the right with his earlier questions. Everything he told us addressed our concerns.

When my wife and I took our turns at the wheel, he moved to the back seat and didn't utter a word. Maybe our driving terrorized the poor guy to a point of speechlessness! That likely wasn't the case—his silence was the next step in a refined process. Without getting into the details of a WOW! delivery, the entire Saturn experience for me was like a breath of fresh air. The reason I purchased this vehicle was, in the end, because of Saturn's sales-training process. Right process, right result.

Nowhere in North America is customer-service training given as much importance as it is at the Container Store in Dallas. In 2000, the Container Store took the top spot on its first entry into *Fortune*'s 100 Best Companies to Work For. To prove it wasn't a fluke, the store took top honors again in 2001. In a segment of the retail sector, where one-hundred-per-cent turnover is commonplace, the Container Store historically turns fifteen to twenty per cent of its staff annually. The reason? Their industry typically offers seven hours of training for first-year, full-time employees. At the Container Store, that number soars to 235 hours.[9]

---

[9] Dottie, Bruce, *30 Days to a Happy Employee,* (Fireside, New York, 2001) pages 156-57.

When I am in front of a prospect who has an interest in my sales, customer-service, or leadership programs, often times they will ask, "What if I train them, and then they leave?" Good Question.

My response? "What if you don't train them, and they stay?"

> *"Acquire new knowledge whilst thinking over the old, and you may become a teacher of others."*
>
> Confucius

Be a Coach

The greatest leaders happen to be, not coincidentally, the best teachers. Call it mentoring, call it teaching, or call it coaching, it boils down to the same thing: the ability to transfer one's knowledge, skills, and values to others. That's why instilling and passing on the culture is so significant. Bill Walsh was one of football's all-time great coaches. His leadership of the San Francisco 49ers is legendary. He took over the coaching reigns of a bumblingly loveable team in 1979. The team was so bad that he couldn't even hire a general manager. With a new philosophy and a leading-edge attitude, he led the 49ers to Super Bowl victories in 1982, 1985, and 1989. His star quarterback, Steve Young, said of Walsh, "Bill hated the way people are treated in football. He made it a people business." What is lost in the shuffle is that besides being a great coach, he was able to mentor his assistant coaches to become great coaches as well. His offensive coordinator, Mike Holmgren, left to become the head coach in Green Bay, where he too coached a Super Bowl winner. When Holmgren was hired, never having held a head coaching position before, he billed himself not as a coach, not as a motivator, but as a *teacher*. Bill Walsh was so able to communicate what was best for his teams that a number of his assistants in addition to Holmgren went on to become head coaches in the NFL, including Jon Gruden, Ray Rhodes, Dennis Green, and Pete Carroll. Like Holmgren and Walsh before that, they see themselves first and foremost as educators.

In business as in sports, mentorship programs are becoming more evident. Enterprise Rent-a-car has developed a mentorship curriculum that sees all of its new management-trainee hires assigned to an experienced mentor who regularly checks the new hire's progress. The result? Enterprise is now the largest car-rental company in North America.

Empower Them

Don't be afraid to let go of the reigns. Ritz Carlton is renowned for empowering its employees to the tune of $2,000 per person to right any customer-service wrongs.

Another company that stresses empowerment, as well as personal accountability, is retailing giant Nordstrom's department stores. Every new hire, as they are welcomed to the team, is given a copy of the following:

Welcome to Nordstrom

We're glad to have you with our company.

Our number-one goal is to provide

Outstanding customer service.

Set both your personal and

Professional goals high.

We have a great confidence in your

Ability to achieve them.

Nordstrom Rules:

Rule #1:
Use your good judgment in all situations.

There will be no additional rules.

Talk about empowering your employees! Not only does the corporation flourish, employees are treated as their own business owners and trusted to do the best for their customers in every situation. The tale of the Nordstrom employee who refunded a customer for a set of winter tires when the store didn't sell winter tires has reached almost folklore proportions. Before you think that Nordstrom is an easy target, the facts are that Nordstrom had purchased the location a short time prior from a company that did sell winter tires. The Nordstrom employee, recognizing that the customer in question may have a strong upside potential for the Nordstrom chain, decided, without intervention on management's behalf, to give the customer a full refund. That's how Nordstrom does business. The top recognizes the power of the front line.

Don Bell, co-founder of Westjet Airlines, has been recognized as being the customer-service architect of the airline. He credits the company's ability to empower its employees to do the right thing for the customer within a loosely defined framework as a major cog in the company's success. "Empowerment is key," he stated. "It is every bit as important as our stock purchase plan. We tie our success to the employees' success." The result is that Westjet is the nation's most profitable airline, and it arrived there in four short years.

Leading a WOW! Customer Service culture is a big responsibility. The leader has to be fully committed and fully accountable to the cause. Leading a WOW! Customer Service culture is not, however, rocket science. True leaders understand the value of their people. Gene Dupuis of Prairie Meats, for example, is proud that his upper-management team earns more than the industry average. He sees them not as employees, but rather as family.

You needn't go that far. However you should be prepared for the inevitable problems and pitfalls that arise from not treating your employees well.

Chapter Five

Happy Employees = Happy Customers

Good Help is Hard to Find...

If you have had to do any amount of hiring, you will know that, no matter your industry, good help is hard to find. Here's a late-breaking news flash—it's even harder to keep.

For some reason, we bend over backwards to hire those we want, then when they become employees, we stop bringing them value as they define it.

An old joke describes this phenomenon aptly: A computer programmer leaves this earth much before his time and is greeted at the Pearly Gates by both St. Peter and the devil. He is offered a choice as to where he wants to spend eternity working, and, to help him with his decision, he is offered a tour of both venues.

His tour of Heaven is very pleasant. The other computer programmers are working diligently, sitting on billowy clouds. Everyone is pleasant and the equipment is state of the art. It is a warm friendly place, and our friend's first impression is that this would be a fine place to spend the rest of eternity.

The devil insists the fellow at least have a look at Hell so that he can make an informed decision. Our hero agrees, and south they go. Hell is not what he had anticipated at all—his favorite rock music is being blasted over top-quality speakers, the coffee breaks are longer than the work periods, and gorgeous scantily clad women bring refreshing cool beverages to the workers on a regular basis.

He returns to the Pearly Gates, regretfully informing St. Peter that, as alluring and friendly as heaven is, his first choice is the other, livelier venue.

He excitedly reports for his first day of work in Hell, and what a shock! The rock music is gone, replaced with a mournful funeral dirge. There are *no* coffee breaks, in fact, lunch is only ten minutes, and the standard workday is sixteen hours. Worse yet, the gorgeous ladies have been replaced by toothless sea hags covered in warts. Instead of

121

bringing the computer whizzes cool drinks, they poke the unsuspecting employees with cattle prods in order to increase productivity. On top of that, the place is hotter than, well, Hell.

At the end of the first workday, he catches up with the devil leaving his office.

"Hey, what's up?!" screams the frazzled programmer. "Yesterday, this place was great. Today it's worse than lousy! How can you explain *that*?"

"It's simple," replied the devil. "Yesterday, you were a prospect, today you're an employee!"

It's funny because it's true. The prospect that we wine and dine today becomes tomorrow's employee #3748. A short time later, employee #3748 feels ignored, abused, and poorly used. Another short period, and employee # 3748 gives notice, willing to go where he feels appreciated. How does this happen? A number of things can go wrong. Our undoing, and our potential employee's undoing, starts in the interview process.

Does the hand fit the glove?
We discussed in Chapter Four the importance of hiring for attitude and training for skill. What *is* the right attitude for the position? If you really like a new prospect's quick wit and charm, but the job calls for superior technical skills and limited interaction with other employees, you have done both your company and the prospect a disservice. Conversely, if the potential new hire has impressed you with technological wizardry but is supposed to be your sales messiah, this match isn't going to have a happy ending either. It is unlikely that either of your new hires will be around to get the twenty-five-year gold watch, or even the ten-month pizza party, unless you can move them into a more suitable position. Their on-the-job frustration will grow, as will yours.

After a period of time, your jaded employees will leave for greener pastures, where their skills will be put to better use. And you will say, "What a lousy employee! They turned out to be so unlike I thought. Good riddance." The fault is not theirs. We can go a long way towards eliminating this type of hiring.

Here's how:

1. Do an in-depth analysis of the job

Long before the first interviewee arrives, do your homework. Determine what the critical success factors are for the position. Know in your own mind the skill sets and personality traits *you* believe would make for an effective employee. This sounds simplistic, but I have been involved on the hiring side of the desk with my cohorts on many occasions and have done interview after interview, waiting for the right interviewee to say and do something that would leave us in awe and simplify the hiring process for us. Not once did we say, "What exactly are we looking for? What qualities would our number-one pick have?" Too many times, we have hired very sharp people—they just weren't right for the job.

Don't be one of those interviewers that has to "sweat" the interviewee just for the sake of doing it. If the largest pressure they're going to have on the job is ensuring the pizza-dough count is correct at shift's end, don't press them for an answer on what they would do if they had spilled hot coffee on the Queen's lap.

2. Ask the people currently doing the job

If you have an employee or employees that are particularly effective at the position, ask them what works and what doesn't. What do they think is the most important trait for the job? How did they get to be successful? Not only will you get a clear picture of what the position really requires, the people you ask will appreciate that they were asked for their input. Asking their opinion gives them more "ownership" in the team.

3. Develop a guide

Develop a list of questions based on the list of qualifications you think are most important, as well as the input of those currently doing the job. If you are hiring for varying positions, develop questions particular to each position. Make a good number of these questions open-ended.

4. Never interview alone

There are a couple of reasons for this. The first is that if you are interviewing a person of the opposite sex, you never want to put yourself in a position where a misunderstood comment can put you where you don't want to be, such as a boiling pot of water! It's tough to win a game of "he said, she said." Eliminate any possibility of that happening. If possible, have at least one person of the same sex as the interviewee in the interview room.

The second reason is to see how the chemistry will be between other individuals and the new hire. Successful sports teams are famous for getting the right chemistry. The feeling is that if they have a group of individuals who care for each other and believe in each other, the team will be more successful.

It's the same in the workplace. You are more apt to have a winning workplace if you let the existing staff have a say in determining their new work partner. Be a little bit innovative and invite an existing employee who is a potential co-worker for the new hire to participate in the interview process. They will know better than you if there is good chemistry. If you are feeling especially innovative, include a prospective subordinate to the prospective new employee in the interview. Let's not lose sight of the fact, though, that while outside input is great, hiring the right person is ultimately your responsibility.

5. Hiring assessment tools

Use these where applicable. They can be very effective, and very telling, but don't let the tool make the final hiring decision. There are some people in the job market that are highly effective at anticipating the kind of answers that the assessment tool wants to hear. In the end, your gut, your guide, and prospective co-workers can offer great insights as to whether or not there is a fit.

6. Clarity

This strikes a chord deep inside me. My former company missed the boat completely on one of our hires, and both the employee and the company came out as losers. The president was quite taken by this young lady, who was technically talented and had an exceptionally creative mind. She was interviewed on four different occasions, once by as many as five people.

Our needs at the time were weighted towards the administrative and technical, but we knew that at some point she would be a great fit for the sales team and told her as much. We said, not clearly enough, that administration, such as booking our travel, keeping in touch with clients, and supporting our office manager technologically, would be her prime responsibilities initially.

She heard, more loudly than we spoke, that we needed sales help. She set about bringing sales ideas and slogans to us on a regular basis. She would ignore booking flights for the sake of coming up with a whizzy new sales slogan. Our office manager, who was already stressed to the max (his huge workload was the reason we hired this person) became even more frazzled. He was doing his old job, trying to train this new person, and doing a portion of her job, all because we weren't clear in the interviews. His workload, already excessive, stretched to the breaking point. Our new hire, envisioning a higher profile and more freedom, soon became restless being cooped up in an office day after day.

It didn't take long for things to go wrong. Hotels and flights not being booked were small prices to pay when compared to the ongoing stress levels at the office. Everyone was mad at everyone. This person didn't fit because we, as potential employers, were not clear in outlining our current needs.

Now I believe firmly that it's not the people you fire that cause you problems; rather, your problems are caused by people you want to fire but don't. This was a tough case because this person was a single mom, and we had lured her away from a secure position where she was successful and respected, to a pressure-cooker environment where she wasn't doing anything near what she wanted. Firing her would have been in our best interests, but how would she fare? To a person, our management team agreed that we had an obligation to her, and we had agreed to tough it out and work with her to get her where she should be focusing her attention. But our problems were alleviated by her giving notice. She had been with us for less than three months, but on both sides it seemed interminable. It was a huge relief to us and, I'm sure to her. She had found a position similar to the one she had left prior to coming to us, where the fit was perfect.

The lessons I learned from that extreme case were many, but mostly I discovered that clarity, letting people know *exactly* what is expected of them, is the only way to go. If their job is to scrub the toilet or bite the heads off of chickens, make sure they are aware of that before they wear their best party dress to that first day on the job.

Clarity means, too, that the new hire is made aware of the company's mission and vision statements. Find time in the hiring process to discover your new hire's personal goals. You can later tie their personal goals to the company's goals. In fairness to your new employee, inform them of any peculiar "political" situations that may come up on the job. Saving them from a possibly embarrassing faux pas will be the first step in establishing yourself as a trustworthy manager.

Be clear about the position's future. It's perfectly natural and acceptable to paint a rosy picture of the company and to what lofty heights the new hire may ascend, but ensure that it is based on historical fact or at least has the possibility of coming true.

Have you ever been the victim of an overzealous recruiter? They tell you that the job has no downside, no risk, and that, as far as income, the sky is the limit. Sure it is, if you work seventeen hours a day, seven days a week, and your closing ratio is eighty-five per cent! When pressed, these recruiters will grudgingly admit that no one has attained the lofty numbers they just told you about so far, but with your talent, attitude, and contacts, you *could* be the first to hit those targets. You didn't appreciate the tall tale, and neither will anyone you exaggerate to in the interview process.

... And harder to keep

The quality of our customer service and the strength of our bottom line often come down to how well we are able to retain our top employees. Sometimes a better offer beckons or they need a new challenge or working for us wasn't all that they thought it would be. Whatever our employees' reasons are for wanting to leave, one thing is certain—they are very expensive to replace.

Multiple research studies have revealed that replacing people costs from seventy to two hundred per cent of the person's annual salary. It is also proven that high-tech workers, professionals, and managers can cost twice as much to replace as other employees. There are a number of hidden costs to consider, such as lost sales due to customers who may follow our former employee to their new place of employment. How do we go about turning new hires into loyal, long-time employees? All we have to do is pay them more than the competition? Right? Wrong.

One of the major factors in employee retention is how the employee feels about their immediate supervisor. A newspaper article by Tag Goulet, appearing in the *Calgary Herald*, quoted a number of interesting points determined by a Gallup Poll. The poll, sampling more than one million employees stated that poorly managed work groups are an average of fifty per cent less productive than well-managed groups. Additionally, if the employee decides to stay and work for the poor manager, there is little chance that the employee will go the extra mile.

The High Cost of Revolving Doors versus Open Doors

If you are anything like me, at some point you have dealt with a company because of the person that serves you. That server is friendly, knowledgeable, and represents themselves and their company enthusiastically. It may be your favorite restaurant or music store or florist. Maybe it's a computer store, where one employee stands head and shoulders above everyone else. If this sounds at all familiar, you may have already discovered a link between your desire to shop where you do and the tenure and attitude of your servers. You will discover that these people are loyal to you and they are loyal to their employer. They are also very valuable to their employer. For example, a study done in the automotive industry revealed that the average cost of replacing a salesperson with between five and eight years of experience with a salesperson of less than one year's experience was as high as $36,000 per month in lost sales.[10] Even more striking is the cost of losing a top-producing stockbroker. It is conservatively estimated that a departed broker with a minimum of five years' experience will cost the firm as much as 2.5 million dollars in lost gross commissions until the point that their replacement broker is up to speed, five years after being hired.

---

[10] Jeffrey J. Zolnitsky, "Making Effective Human Resource Management a Hard Business Issue" *Compensation and Benefits Management,* Winter 1995, pages 16-24.

What can you do about retention?
If you're a manager and you can't help but notice that productivity and morale in your team are low and your staff turnover numbers rival that of lemmings heading for the cliffs, fear not! There are things you can do to turn things around—and turn them around quickly.

No one sets out to be a lousy manager. There is a good chance that your promotions through the ranks were based on skills that aren't applicable to where you are today. You may have started on the technical or accounting side of the business, and since you were so exceptional in those areas, you were rewarded with the position of manager or vice president, where suddenly you were expected to know about (gulp!) people. If this sounds like you, there are thousands more like you out there. If your company hasn't sponsored you to take an applicable course, re-reading the section on teamwork in this chapter will be a good start.

Self-knowledge
Great leadership begins with taking the time to get to know and understand yourself. If you want to be a great manager of men and women, spend a little time alone with nothing but your thoughts. What kind of person are you, really? Do you lead by example? Are you able to spur your troops on to greater deeds through your inspirational words? Have you even earned the right to lead them at all? Most importantly, how does your team view you? Remember, the teams with the lowest morale and worst productivity are headed by people who are viewed as (there's no nice way to say this) jerks, weasels, or butt-heads by the people they lead. Now this may not sound like you to *you,* but let's do a quick self-appraisal to see if you are guilty of any of these offenses:

- Withholding information so you alone "hold the power"
- Swearing
- Criticizing staff in front of others

129

- ❑ Talking down to staff
- ❑ Acting in an arrogant manner
- ❑ Intimidating staff
- ❑ Taking credit for the work and ideas of staff
- ❑ Being sexist or racist
- ❑ Giving feedback that is only negative
- ❑ Not listening
- ❑ Having two sets of rules, one for you, one for your team
- ❑ Frequently and suddenly bursting into anger
- ❑ Seeing yourself as a cop, not a coach
- ❑ Taking your lousy mood out on your staff
- ❑ Setting unreal expectations and deadlines for your staff

How did you do?

If none of the above sounds like you, you have greatness in you and will likely be respected, if not revered, by your team. Don't get too cocky, though; there are a lot more words that have negative connotations for leaders, and if we looked long enough, we would find some. The main thing here is that you are on the right track, and if you are willing to learn and are committed to your staff, you will become an even more effective leader.

If you have exhibited one to three of these characteristics, you are not perfect, but by recognizing your faults you should be able to fix them on your own. You are viewed as a tough manager, but your team is willing to overlook your shortcomings because you have an even longer list of positives.

If you showed four or five of these traits, you should consider taking a management course or a course on anger management. You are not great, but you still have the capacity to lead and manage, albeit with help. Your shortcomings at this point will have a negative impact on morale, productivity, and retention.

If you exhibited more than five of these traits, you are not meant to lead in today's marketplace. This style of leadership may have had a place in the Civil War, but I doubt even that. You are either an incompetent who hates the job you are in or a bully who loves it because you get to spend your entire workweek pushing people around. Your team's efforts will be lagging and your retention numbers accordingly low. The best advice I could give would be

    a)   Hire someone to test your food and drink at work before you try it, and

    b)   If the person you hire survives the food, have them start your car for you at day's end.

If you have ever had the experience of working for a cretin like this, you'll know that not all of what I say is tongue in cheek. The best paying job I had until my current career was a sales position with a world-class firm, which was ended by me because of just such a person.

The company, a Fortune 500 company, was known for its technological innovation. Our regional sales manager was a former technician who ascended to his position because he was an effective, even excellent, technician. He knew nothing about people. I remember to this day the anguished anticipation of our weekly telephone sales meeting. My stomach would develop a major knot, and I could feel the tension mount as I faxed our team's weekly sales projections and results to him. Our appointed time was 11:00 a.m. every Friday morning. As much as we hated those meetings starting on time, you'd know that if his incoming call came later than that time, the other branches were *really* getting it, and we could expect a rough ride. The meetings were highlighted (or lowlighted) by brow-beating, bullying, insulting, and intimidating tactics. Pity the poor team member who forecast business that didn't come in. That person was singled out for a special brand of abuse that featured derogatory name-calling and possibly ancestral insult. Worse yet was making a sale that you hadn't forecast. "Don't you pussies even know what the hell's happening in your territories? Useless bastards!" It just never left me with a warm, fuzzy.

If payday happened to fall on a Friday, we would head to a lounge in the area, often accompanied by members of the technical team. We would relate the tales of our recent verbal beatings to them over a beer and nachos as they listened incredulously. Prior to one o'clock, the techs would get up and return to work. Not the sales guys. We would stay and lick our wounds, arguing who got it the worst this time and who next week's big loser was bound to be. This was hardly a productive use of our time and we knew it. It was, in part, a defense mechanism and, in part, a way to extract revenge. This was in the days before everyone carried a pager and a cell phone everywhere they went, and often our regional manager would have a reason to call one of us in the office on a Friday afternoon. No one home. I'm sure he thought that he had motivated us sufficiently to end our week making cold calls. In fact, we would be on our second plate of nachos and third pitcher of beer! One of the other salespeople at the branch, at the time a twenty-four-year-old talent, was so disturbed by this Friday morning terror that he developed an ulcer. After he had taken all the abuse he could with us, he left to take a lesser-paying job, just to escape the unnecessary pressure. With a little positive coaching and some respect, he was able to turn his career around. Today, he is a star performer, often the top sales performer in his company, regularly winning incentives and trips abroad. Oh, by the way, he thinks his current sales manager is great. I have met his sales manager and have done some customer-service work for the company. He confided in me that he doesn't have all the answers but listens to his team, treats them with respect, and acts as their coach. It seems to be working.

Our old regional sales manager? He was fired not long after I left. It seems his region's sales production wasn't what it should have been, and his retention was the worst in the country. It was a few years after I left that I discovered every sales team in the region had the same Friday payday ritual—get abused, extend lunch, let the sales slide for today. It was another lesson for me. The people that I am asked to lead today are treated with the utmost respect. We still have differences, but the communication and respect go both ways.

Feed them the right information
Today's workplace is not what we were led to believe it would be. In the early nineties we were told to expect four-day workweeks, shortened hours, and job-sharing. Even with these appealing features, we were to make the same amount of money as we already were, and we were to live happily ever after. So, what happened? Today, as a society, we are working longer and harder than our parents did following the end of the Second World War. There is more stress and depression in the workplace than at any other point in history. We keep our noses to the grindstone and work until the day is done. This in itself is not bad.

It begins to break down when, because of time constraints, we cease to share needed information with out staff. We are too busy, or they are too busy, to meet and share. Being too busy, though, is no excuse for not sharing information. Just as with external customers, you have to keep your staff in the loop. If no information is forthcoming, employees will *invent it*. It's like starting a story on one side of a crowded room. The story is repeated and changed, repeated and changed, so that when it gets back to the start, it bears no resemblance to the original story. If you don't want to hear the water-cooler rumor that the local operation will be closing and moved to Bangladesh, then keep your staff informed.

In the absence of regular informational meetings, share with your staff through short e-mails and memos. If you are legitimately too busy for even that, catch them at a lunch or coffee break and bring them up to speed. Meet with them walking the same direction in the hallway. As long as the information is pertinent to them, it's a good thing to do.

Sharing information builds trust, given that the information is right for the people with whom you are sharing. Never, under any circumstances, even if your team is dying for information, divulge to them information not intended for them or told to you in confidence.

Address Political Realities

Most companies have within their framework cultural and political realities that only exist in that company. As addressed earlier in this chapter, discuss these realities (or peculiarities) openly and honestly with your team. Save them from any possible gaffes or embarrassing statements by giving them a heads-up as to who may sport hidden agendas or is liable to go over their heads or is likely to repeat what has been told in confidence. In other words, offer a little bit of protection.

The same is true for the company's strategic direction. Make sure the team knows the vision and mission statements. Let them know well in advance how new trends and technologies may affect their careers. Who wouldn't rather hear today that they may want to consider building some new job skills as their current position may be redundant in a year than be told in a year that their job is obsolete? Be honest, be fair.

You will be surprised that when you begin to share information in a positive light, useful positive information flowing from the team to you will increase. Shared information leads to trust, which leads to improved job satisfaction, which leads to improved retention.

Respect

The workplace has changed so much in the past fifteen years as to be almost unrecognizable. We have to be so concerned with political correctness and people's rights that we wonder what happened to their responsibilities. There are times when we are chastised for using humor in the workplace for fear it will offend someone. If we let it, our workplace will become a drier, less enjoyable place to spend our most productive hours.

We have on our teams today such a mix of colors, religions, geographic backgrounds, and sexual preferences that we have to walk on eggshells in order not to offend. All of this stuff is basically nonsense, if you bear in mind one little word—*respect*. Treat people the way they want to be treated. Treat them with dignity. Recognize that a number of them are different from you. Respect that difference, even celebrate that difference.

Accountability

Make no mistake, retention is the responsibility of *everyone* in the organization. Gone are the days of dumping the challenge of holding onto employees on the plate of the human-resource department. This isn't to say that the human-resource department doesn't play a major role, because obviously it does, in running necessary programs and acting as a liaison between the team and management. What matters most, though, is the direct relationship between manager and employee. As much as fifty per cent of work life satisfaction is directly attributable to the relationship between the employee and the manager. Accept the fact that you—yes, you, Mr. or Ms. Department head or Supervisor— are as important to retention as all of the other factors combined.

Treat Them Well

Here's a fact that too many employers either don't know or don't care about: Companies that tend to kick around their team players, their internal customers, will have team players that tend to kick around their external customer. Conversely, companies that treat team members well will have team members that treat the external customer like royalty! Don't believe me? Have a look at Southwest Airlines' mission statement.

The Mission of Southwest Airlines

The mission of Southwest Airlines is dedication to the highest quality of Customer Service delivered with a sense of warmth, friendliness, individual pride, and Company Spirit.

To Our Employees

We are committed to provide our employees a stable work environment with equal opportunity for learning and personal growth.

Creativity and innovation are encouraged for improving the effectiveness of Southwest Airlines. Above all, employees will be provided the same concern, respect, and caring attitude with the organization that they are expected to share externally with every Southwest Customer.

The first thing that struck me when I read it was the fact that more emphasis was placed on the team than on the external customer. The second thing that struck me was the fact that the words "Customer" and "Service" were capitalized. This is a company that truly cares for its people, and the results are staggering. From entry-level training, where exercises such as the Crocodile River training exercise, which calls for total cooperation to cross an imaginary river, to charitable activities, where over half of Southwest's staff work together, the importance of teamwork is stressed. The end result is that teamwork has allowed Southwest Airlines to turn their planes in less than half the time of the industry average, resulting in the highest percentage of profit in the airline industry. Everyone pitches in, from pilots who help to load luggage or clean the cabin after the last passenger has de-planed to a CEO that helps baggage handlers load planes every Thanksgiving. Teamwork has played an enormous role in making Southwest Airlines the most profitable airline in North America. They boast a record of twenty-eight consecutive years of profitability, a statistic unparalleled in the industry.

Denis and Muntener Advertising Ltd., of Prince George, British Columbia, is another shining example of a company's commitment to teamwork. President Dan Denis is as creative as they come when dealing with clients and prospects. He and partners Roman Muntener and Carol Fairhurst have channeled that same creativity to their team.

Most months, team players are given the responsibility of arranging an activity that the rest of the team will enjoy. The office shuts down for an afternoon and, en masse, they descend upon a venue, to enjoy camaraderie, while pushing their personal boundaries, just as they are expected to do at work.

Some of their activities are laid back and easy to do, such as an eight ball and pizza party at a local billiard hall or a tour of a new art gallery. Other team-building activities can be a bit more rigorous, such as laser tag or ten-pin bowling or mountain hiking. Other suggestions include a jet-boat river ride or horseback riding. Each and every activity undertaken has formed a closer bond on an already close team.

Staff turnover has been virtually non-existent for the last five years. This is rare in an industry where the staff is under the ongoing pressure of meeting daily deadlines and bringing new and creative ideas to their clients.

As Dan Denis will tell you, this doesn't happen by accident. "Every year employees do an evaluation of the workplace. They are expected to complete a homework assignment which consists of a four to five hour questionnaire on how we can improve on what we do, both internally and externally. Our morale is excellent and our entire staff of ten get along like they were family!"

On this team, birthdays are recognized with a gift, and the entire team goes out for an extended lunch.

Their most successful outing, though, is their annual Live Theatre Appreciation Night. All year, they give preferential treatment to and sponsor the local theatre group. Then, one night a year, the theatre group will respond in kind by performing one of its mainstage productions for Denis and Muntener. Never one to miss an opportunity, Dan will invite existing clients to this performance, which includes wine and cheese. Just prior to the performance, each team member is introduced to the audience. The audience is then told how this particular team member contributes to the overall good of the clients.

Talk about win/win! Clients are treated to a great night of entertainment, and Denis and Muntener staff are treated like a good-will sandwich, being shown appreciation from two sides.

As successful as that event is, they have incorporated yet another staff appreciation event. In 2000 they sponsored their first business exchange. Andrea Walker, a graphic designer, traded places with a Swiss graphic designer. For seven weeks they lived in each other's apartments, drove each other's cars, and, most importantly, performed each other's jobs.

"It was a great experience, performing the same job in a different atmosphere," said Walker. "In North America we make things so complex, whereas the European designs are simplistic and practical. In the past week alone I have had four clients accept my Web design proposals. Each one of those designs was based on European models."

In addition to the personal experience, Walker appreciates the value that her contributions make to the team. "The company is very proactive in allowing us learning opportunities. As individuals we are given the freedom to explore opportunities that we feel would be beneficial to both ourselves and the company. Then, as a team, we decide whether there is merit in proceeding. It certainly makes you feel valued."

Front-line servers are not involved in designing the program.
The input of one of our two most important groups, our front-line staff, is overlooked. Instead of garnering that invaluable information, a tall forehead with more education than the front-line server but zero hands-on experience is called in to save the day. There's no buy-in from the front-line staff, and the program that is designed may not even address the needs of the customer.

Customers aren't consulted.
When we design our whizzy slogans and programs, sometimes we don't spend a millisecond considering our customers' needs.

Here's a classic example. A few years back, Greyhound instituted a computerized operating system called "Trips." Like so many companies, downsizing and cutbacks of staff and routes had led to the decline in the level of Customer Service at Greyhound. Enter "Trips," a way to regain credibility and increase efficiency. The thought on the street, especially Wall Street, was that improved scheduling and a sophisticated reservation system would elevate bus travel standards to the same level as air travel. Wall Street was even more impressed when the share price of

Greyhound's shares almost doubled in the six-month period after "Trips" was announced.

Then came reality. Not long after the system was operational, the share price plummeted on the news that ridership had fallen twelve per cent in one month. Whoops! What could possibly have gone wrong?

For starters, the company wasn't great at implementing a computerized system. Destinations weren't included in the database, a keystroke could take up to forty-five seconds to register, followed by a five-minute wait to have a ticket printed. Sometimes computer-generated glitches would see people stranded in terminals. Sometimes lucky passenger that caught the right bus to the right destination had luggage that wasn't so lucky; it ended up in another town or state.

The big thing, though, was that Greyhound didn't stop to question if that was what their passengers wanted or needed. You see, bus riders earn, on average, seventeen thousand dollars a year. A lot of them don't have credit cards to book a trip in advance, even if they wanted to. For them, the old system worked fine. On rare occasions when the bus they wanted to take was full, they would wait for the next one or come back later. As it turned out, Trips was not necessary, except as an example of how it's important to include your customers in decisions that affect them.[11]

Customer-Service Teams and Working Styles

It's a flashback! We talked in Chapter Three about the importance of client communication standards, and how powerful it is to understand why your clients react to certain situations as they do, and how you can communicate with them in a manner they relate to. It is the same with customer-

[11] Richard Whiteley and Diane Hessan, *Customer Centered Growth,* (Adison-Wesley Publishing 1996) page 34.

service teams. Every member of the team is distinct, there is no one else like them. How many managers have you seen, though, that tend to motivate each individual using the identical method? There are some people who stand up well to tough talk, but there are a lot fewer that stand up to public criticism, which sends a few running from the room in tears. For the record, I have never been a proponent of public criticism. The way to build trust and foster respect in people is not by ripping them to shreds in front of an audience.

Power of WOW! Customer Service is more apt to be evident in companies where all team members' contributions are recognized and appreciated. Every team, from size three to size fourteen, is made up of individuals with totally different personality types. The key to making teams work is to recognize, then capitalize, on each of those different personality types.

The topic of Personality Styles is being revisited from Chapter Three under teamwork, because that's where Power of WOW! Customer Service begins. The fact of the matter is, though, that your knowledge and use of Personality Styles with your external customers will have a huge impact on setting you above, not apart from, the rest of the pack. So let's look at Personality Styles as they pertain to our internal customers (our team), but make sure you use it every day with your external customers (Chapter Three).

Nowhere is effective implementation of Personality Styles more crucial than in the workplace. Good use of Personality Styles can make poor workplace relationships good and good workplace relationships better.

At their best, workplaces are their own vibrant, cooperative, functional communities. At worst they are teeming cauldrons of discontent, where finger-pointing, backstabbing, and stress are the order of the day. What is truly sad is that it may take something as simple as knowing how to interact with one another, by getting in lockstep with others who are not like us, to turn the tables. It could be something as simple as knowing Personality Styles and recognizing why some individuals react to specific events in a specific manner.

Most companies will have a variety of Personality Styles on board, and some gravitate to certain positions by their very nature. Before I get accused of stereotyping, though, let me say that no matter your Personality Style, you can be whatever you want to be, *if* you want to be. Typically, however, here is what happens:

Amiables tend to gravitate to the helping professions. They are at their best as teachers, nurses, physiotherapists; and you see them everywhere in the hospitality industry. They want to be in a position to help others. They also excel as managers of first impressions, usually receptionists, or call-center customer service representatives. They genuinely care about their teammates and customers as people.

Analyticals usually meander along a path that leads them towards thinking professions, where interpersonal contact is minimal. Professions like accounting, engineering, and computers are where they normally shine. While personal interaction isn't a must for them, they can be effective. They shine, though, in that they have an uncanny ability to solve technical problems, and since they like to work alone, they are usually low-maintenance workers.

Expressives will lean towards professions where they are constantly on display, and they are able to capitalize on their flamboyance. Careers such as acting, sometimes teaching, training, or facilitating would be their natural habitats. Because of their ability to persuade others, you also see them as salespeople in many industries. They are popular in the workplace because they bring fun and energy to the work-a-day world.

Drivers can be found anywhere in an organization, but they usually rise to the top, or close to it, not because of their people skills, but rather because of their ambition and focus. You will see them as presidents of many companies and, for that matter, countries. You may also find them as doctors and lawyers.

As you can see, the potential for workplace explosions and implosions are many. The Expressive salesperson can't understand why the Analytical accountant won't extend more credit to a customer who is ninety days overdue, when the salesperson did a bang-up presentation to make the sale.

The Analytical accountant can't for a second fathom why the Expressive salesperson made the call in the first place. Didn't she know company policy?

And the Amiable receptionist can't understand why the Driver president snapped at her about the high-priority package not being shipped yesterday afternoon, when she never received it until this morning. Being Amiable, she says nothing.

The Driver president, concerned with budgets, hiring a new V.P. of finance, and ensuring that the new quality-assurance program is implemented on time, doesn't even notice that the receptionist is upset. "That package should have been sent yesterday," he thinks to himself.

Sure, the opportunities for miscommunication are rampant, but so are the opportunities to build a more harmonious team atmosphere.

Before proceeding, though, it's best to inform you that this can only work if individual team members have both the knowledge and the commitment. Like most things in this book the ideas put forth will only garner positive results if they are put into action.

The use of Personality Styles is meant to build trust, not to trick people. Without being a phony, try to be just a little more like your teammate. They trust people who are like themselves, just as you tend to trust people that are like you.

Here's how Personality Styles *can* work on teams:

For Amiables Only

A. Interacting with Analytical Teammates

1) Be punctual for meetings
By and large, the clock is much more important to Analyticals than Amiables. Respect their time, and never be late for a meeting. A very annoying thing for an Analytical is to hear an Amiable chatting merrily with another teammate, while the Analytical checks the clock, noting the minutes or seconds that the Amiable is late for their meeting. And, yes, they will know the minutes *and* seconds.

2) Don't just be seen as a visitor
Get down to business and stay down to business. The Analytical will care nothing about little Sarah's dance class or that you bowled a perfect game. There is not much chance that the Analytical will share much of their personal life with you. If they do, it's a bonus. They trust you implicitly. Take what they give you and treat it with respect. Never pry.

3) Talk about 'thinking' as opposed to 'feeling'
The Analytical will feel at ease with the word 'think.' Feeling-type words will give them an uneasy feeling. As Amiables, supportive, friendly conversation is the norm. Add more formal words and actions to your interactions with Analyticals. Words like 'objective' or 'plan' or 'analysis' are good to work into to your conversations. Limit your gestures a little.

4) Respect their space
Part of the Analytical's behavior pattern is to have little piles of paper everywhere. Typically, their workplace is organized chaos. Never, under any circumstances move one of those

piles of paper. Ask them to move the pile or ask permission to move it.

Respect their personal space, too. Amiables are great 'touchers.' Analyticals are lousy 'touchees.' Touching an Analytical teammate, other than pushing them out of the way of an oncoming vehicle, is a no-no.

B. Interacting with Expressive Teammates

1) Speak and move more quickly than you normally would

Expressives are usually more energized than Amiables, so in your interactions, speed everything up a notch. Eliminate as many pauses as you can from your speech. Increase eye contact.

2) Let them know what you want

Amiables are famous for putting their wants into question form, for example, an Amiable spouse might ask, "Do you feel we need new dining-room furniture?" when they want new furniture. Similarly, in the workplace they might ask, "We're so far behind right now. Do you think we should put the Phelps project on the back burner?" With an Expressive, the Amiable has to step up, and be a little more assertive; "Because we are so far behind, I feel it would be in everyone's best interest to put the Phelps project on the back burner."

Use the 'language of leadership.' Drop tentative words and phrases. Words like 'I'll try,' 'I guess,' and 'as soon as possible' should be replaced with 'I will,' 'I feel,' and 'it will be ready by four o'clock, Tuesday.'

3) Accept 'hurry up and wait'

The project, as seen by the Expressive, is the Most Important Thing in the Universe! As a supportive and cooperative Amiable, you bust your hump to get it done in world-record time. Then it sits and sits, gathering dust for possibly months. As an Amiable, you aren't likely to confront the Expressive, so you fester and stew. You are likely to become less cooperative than usual towards this individual. So accept that it will happen at some point, and don't let it get to you. When the Expressive tires of the current flavor of the month, your project will get it's due.

4) Discuss fewer issues than you want to
Take your original list of things you want to address, and eliminate about a third. Meet more often, with fewer topics. Ensure that your interactions have an element of fun.

C. Interacting with Driver Teammates

1) Accelerate your pace
Move quickly, meet quickly, and leave quickly. You don't want to be late for this get-together, either.

2) Implement any decisions in a timely manner
Drivers are a 'why wasn't it done yesterday?' kind of people. When they say that it should be done 'as soon as possible,' that means as soon as you get back to your workstation. They are results driven, which runs counter to the Amiable's mindset, so respect that.

3) Use 'thinking' as opposed to 'feeling'
As with Analyticals, the more words you can use like 'focus,' 'plan,' 'objectives,' and 'proof,' the more positive your interaction will be. Also, like Analyticals, they are lousy 'touchees.' The only difference is that their reaction to that misdemeanor may be more intense.

4) Be prepared, be organized
You will be expected to make good use of the time allotted. Have notes prepared, and it's a good idea to have an agenda.

Don't pull ideas out of a hat. If you have 'the greatest idea since sliced bread' type of idea during the meeting, put it on the agenda for the next time.

5) Offer options
It doesn't matter whether you are an Amiable dealing with a Driver, or any other Personality Style dealing with a Driver, one of their hot buttons is control. The only way to accomplish that is to give them options. Give them two, or three at the maximum.

D. Interacting with Other Amiables

The danger of two Amiables working together is that while the relationship will feature cooperation and support, it will also feature a good deal of visiting back and forth, decreasing productivity.

The best solution would be if one of the parties steps even temporarily into the role of another Personality Style, so that objectives and timelines are adhered to.

Greatest Strengths They Bring to a Team
Their willingness to support others is their greatest asset to the team. Amiables are good listeners and have a strong sense of teamwork.

However, their reluctance to confront their teammates when they feel they have been wronged could potentially lead to a festering resentment that could cause them to withdraw their support from the team or direct some of that resentment to the co-worker at a later date.

For Analyticals Only

A. Interacting with Amiable Teammates

1) Make more eye contact than you normally would

As an Analytical, you are least likely of the Personality Styles to care about eye contact. Amiables, being the most sociable of the Personality Styles like frequent but not ongoing eye contact. Make an effort to connect occasionally. It's fine to disconnect for a while, but come back often, if only for a few seconds, to 'look 'em in the eye.'

2) Let down your personal guard

Amiables love to socialize. They are guaranteed to ask you personal questions at coffee or lunch breaks, even passing in hallways, or while loading a truck. Even though it's uncomfortable, let them in a little. Share something personal, even a small thing with them.

3) Let them know that you care

The greatest need an Amiable has is approval. As an Analytical, you tend to be more of a perfectionist. That means that when you catch them doing something right, let them know. Since neither of you likes the limelight, thank them one on one. Your perfectionist side means that you are quick to criticize. Back off a little on the criticism, and when you must find fault with their performance, do so constructively.

4) Your loyalty will be returned and then some

Amiables are the sorts of people who will go to the wall for co-workers, subordinates, supervisors, and the organization if they feel those organizations are loyal to them. Who am I kidding? If they feel loyalty, they will go *through* the wall and through the gates of hell for people they feel support them fully. A word of caution though: while showing them loyalty, never 'slag' anyone else. All of that loyalty will be up in a puff of smoke if they view you as a critical gossip.

B. Interacting with Expressive Teammates

1) Allow them to be the life of the workplace party

When you check your Contact Management System, and it calls for you to begin the next project with your Expressive teammate at 10:15 a.m., you are always put out when they show up at 10:18 and begin the meeting by joking around. Rather than being aloof, or criticizing them, go along for the ride for a while. You don't have to try to reciprocate, an Expressive likely wouldn't appreciate your brand of humor anyway. If you think it's getting overdone, without confrontation, begin the project on your own. If they still persist in joking as opposed to working let them know without being critical or sarcastic that you would really appreciate their help.

2) Exhibit more energy than usual

Expressives are usually very energetic, you not so. Shift it up a gear. Speak a bit faster than normal, walk more quickly, and exhibit a few gestures that are just a little out of the box for you.

3) Let them know you care

Expressives are similar to Amiables in that they like to be shown appreciation, only more so. Way more so. In fact they thrive on appreciation. They differ from Amiables in that the appreciation should be shown publicly, at a formal meeting, or at least informally in front of their peers. It's okay to show appreciation for the same thing more than once.

4) Ease up on the facts, data, and logic

You are driven by facts, data and logic. Expressives are not. You will build more trust with them more quickly if you are able to eliminate any facts not pertinent to your case. The Expressive really only needs the information to look, sound, and feel good in order to make a decision; so don't mire them in detail. That's when they begin to roll their eyes.

C. Interacting with Driver Teammates

1) Increase the eye contact

It might seem that the Driver across the table is trying to bore a hole in your head with her laser-eye contact, but do your best to match that unblinking gaze. Hold your ground, and your eye contact. If you can, make a bet-I-can-go-longer-without-blinking game of it!

2) You know a lot of 'stuff'

The Driver, though, won't be overly impressed by that. Lose some of the detail that normally pervades your speech. Be brief and to the point. Use details only if asked.

3) Be more proactive than usual

Drivers are results-driven people. You will be forgiven if you produce a great deal of work that you view as less than beneficial. The Driver may view the effort as progress, even though you think otherwise. Don't downplay your efforts.

D. Dealing with Other Analyticals

Let's face it, the information to come out of an interaction between Analyticals will be one hundred per cent accurate, the 't's will be crossed and the 'i's will be dotted. However, it may take a long time to complete a project.

Even though Analyticals aren't noted for having strong opinions, their overwhelming desire to be right could lead to potential conflict over who is the most right!

As with the other styles, an ideal situation would have one of the Analyticals stepping into the role of another style so that the human side of the project is not overlooked and deadlines are met.

Greatest Strengths They Bring to the Team
The Analytical style has great problem-solving abilities. They will find the best, most logical solution to a problem. They are "low-maintenance" in that they work very well on their own. I would also include the fact that they are skeptical as a strength. They don't rush into a decision without putting a lot of thought into it. They pay keen attention to detail.

Since Analyticals respond better to fact than emotion, they are sometimes seen as being aloof by some of their teammates. One of their greatest strengths, their attention to detail, is also one of their biggest weaknesses. This occurs when they are put under pressure. They will tend to overanalyze a situation, causing delays and stress for other members of the team.

For Expressives Only

A. Interacting with Amiable Teammates

1) Slow it down
By and large, Expressives speak more quickly than Amiables. In order to connect, try to speak and move a bit more slowly than you normally would. It's in your best interests, too, to ask more and talk less. The Amiable wants to get along with you, and they have a story or example that they want to share with you. Give them the opening.

2) Paraphrase back what you heard

This enables you to understand the Amiable's point of view without agreeing or disagreeing. If you do have to disagree or criticize, do so gently, or you will force them into a shell. This isn't a great idea if you value their input on an ongoing basis.

3) Let them know you appreciate their efforts

Like you, the Expressive, Amiables like to hear they are appreciated. Do so often, but not publicly. In their minds, if you are praising them publicly, why aren't you praising Analytical Al publicly as well? He did good work, too. Amiables cringe when thrust into the spotlight.

4) Negotiate a joint solution

Amiables are used to getting steamrolled, but just because they are used to it doesn't mean they like it. Rather than imposing your will on them, do your best to arrive at a win/win solution. They will appreciate that they were heard.

B. Interacting with Analytical Teammates

1) Don't rush them

Unless you are operating under a really tight timeline, give Analyticals leeway with deadlines. Their number-one desire is to get things right. As an Expressive who wants things done right now as opposed to done right, allow them the time it takes to ensure that they are indeed correct.

2) Get them involved in the conversation

Develop some open-ended questions that will involve them. "I would like to hear what you think of this approach" or "How does this fit with your concept of what we're doing?" may be the starter that you need. When you ask this type of question, prepare for a lot of detail!

3) When making a point, lean back

For the most part, this is how they will act when making a point, so it's best to act in the same fashion. When you do lean back it also naturally decreases your intensity level. This means your gaze is less intense, your gestures less emphatic. All of these things will increase the Analytical's comfort level.

4) Set high standards, follow through

Analyticals set high work standards for themselves and expect the same of others. When working with Analyticals, resist the urge to say "That'll do" or "Close enough." Those statements may be true for an Expressive but will miss the mark with an Analytical.

When setting work standards for yourself, make sure you do what you say. Losing that credibility will result in a rapid disconnect from the Analytical.

C. Interacting with Driver Teammates

1) Express thoughts over feelings

Appeal to the logic of the Driver by articulating thoughts rather than sharing feelings.

2) Expect them to be impersonal

While Expressives and Drivers share similarities from an assertiveness standpoint, there is little commonality in the responsiveness. Don't be put off when the Drivers in your workplace come off as aloof and emotionally detached. Accept it, and don't take it personally. While you may view them as aloof and uncommunicative, there is nothing to be gained from lapsing into your best jokes or impressions of famous people to get them on your side.

3) Set realistic work goals and deadlines

As an Expressive, you are a cockeyed optimist. Drivers on your teams are straight-shootin' realists. Be enthusiastic, be optimistic, but make sure the figures and deadlines that you set are attainable when they affect a Driver.

4) Provide hard, verifiable data

If your task is to win a Driver over to your side, don't do so using hearsay or opinions. You will only convince them with measurable, factual data. Expect to be challenged.

D. Interacting with Other Expressives

The positive aspect of a workplace relationship between two Expressives is that there will be a lot of energy and there should be a lot of laughs. The downside is that two Expressives will give little attention to necessary details, especially details encompassing others. If our Expressives are both really assertive, a pushing contest could break out as to who gets their name mentioned first, who gets the most credit, etc.

It would be best if one of our Expressives were willing to step into a more detail-driven style.

Greatest Strengths They Bring to the Team

Expressives are wonderful leaders because of their ability to persuade others. They can make a work environment fun. Co-workers see them as enthusiastic people, who are enjoyable to be with.

When this happens, however, the less flamboyant team members want the Expressive to put a sock in it and quit showing off! When they are criticized, they may lash out verbally and cause some friction on the team. It should also be noted that they are *not* big on details!

For Drivers Only

A. Interacting with Amiable Teammates

1) Talk about more than work
Capitalize on breaks in meetings or coffee or lunch breaks to introduce a topic that isn't work related. This will be a stretch, but the Amiable will appreciate the effort.

2) Stroke them a little
While Drivers don't need a lot of positive reinforcement, Amiables thrive on it. It would be at the top of an Amiable's list to give an 'atta boy' or 'atta girl.' As a Driver make a concentrated effort to give the Amiables on your team some strokes from time to time. At the same time, decrease the amount of criticism you normally level towards them or others.

3) Give the Amiable clear guidelines
The Amiable has not been blessed with good planning skills. When possible, give them crystal-clear processes to follow. Every once in a while, pitch in on a project that's giving them stress.

B. Interacting with Expressive Teammates

1) Talk about others
The ever-inquisitive Expressive is forever wondering what's going on with other team members. Share a little of what you know about what's going on with people you know. This isn't meant to gossip, but rather to keep them in the loop.

2) Be prepared for meetings to take longer than usual

The Expressive can be a verbal pinball, bouncing from one topic to another. Go into a meeting expecting that the timelines may have to expand a little to accommodate all of the Expressive's verbal meanderings.

3) Show them you care

The largest need that an Expressive has is appreciation. Catch them doing something right, and compliment them. The best place to compliment them is in front of an audience of their peers. They thrive on being made to look good. If you don't risk losing control, let them tell their own story.

4) Let them roam a little

Expressives don't handle being chained to a desk as well as you do. When it's possible, find a reason to move the meeting, view something off-site, or have a meeting in a hallway. If the meeting will be held in one main location, allow them time to move around from time to time, so they are able to expend some energy.

C. Dealing with Analyticals

1) Lose some bluster, Buster

The Analytical will have a hard time keeping up with you. Don't talk as loud as usual, don't talk as fast as usual, and work a few pauses into your verbal communications. In short, soften it up a little.

2) Ease up on the eye contact

Make sure you don't overpower the Analytical with your steady gaze. They will feel more comfortable if you disconnect from time to time, then reconnect.

3) Give them the downside of your ideas
Analyticals are used to being told what Drivers 'want,' and how the Driver's ideas should be implemented. To build trust with an Analytical, allow that you don't have all the best ideas and that your ideas have some identifiable problems.

4) Be accurate
Drivers aren't detail driven, while Analyticals are painstakingly accurate. When dealing with Analyticals, make sure you have all of the details accounted for before you open your mouth.

D. Dealing with Other Drivers

Nowhere is the potential for fireworks greater than when two or more Drivers are working on a project. Each is assertive, each has strong opinions, and each is crystal clear as to the outcome they want. As with the other styles, one should assume some of the characteristic of another Personality Style, so that details and the human side of business are taken care of.

To avoid Driver-to-Driver conflict at work, take it upon yourself to lighten up on the intensity, and become a little more malleable. It doesn't mean that you lost or that you're becoming 'squishy.' It means that you put the company's success ahead of your ego, and that's not a bad thing.

Greatest Strengths They Bring to the Team
They will take charge and get a lot of things accomplished in a short period of time. In a team setting, you always know where they stand—they have no hidden agenda. They do well in positions of authority.

Drivers sometimes don't relate well to others because their personalities are so strong. They may hurt feelings without even being aware of it. They are not detail people. Since they are so competitive, they may have a hard time leaving work at the end of the day. These people have the potential to become workaholics.

You can't improve morale by decree, and you can't build a caring customer-service team through intimidation. You can't force your employees or co-workers to love their jobs. You can, however, foster an attitude and build a culture with cornerstones of mutual respect and caring. You can treat them in the same manner that you would like to see them treat your customers. Most will respond in kind—not all—just the ones you want to keep.

Those that buy in will buy in lock, stock, and barrel. They will promote the company's values and live the company's culture. They will accept and expect training to make them better employees, better co-workers, and better people all around. They are the future core of the company.

A rare few will take it to the next level. These people will do whatever it takes to prove to the customer how valuable they are. They will exude caring and empathy. They are the future leaders of the company. These are the few that will pay close attention to the little things that separate the winners from the also-rans.

Chapter Six

Little Things Make
A Big Difference

> "If you care at all, you'll get some results. If you care enough, you'll get incredible results."
>
> Jim Rohn

Imagine this scenario: It's 6:55 a.m. You pull out of your driveway already ten minutes late for a meeting, and you can't help but notice that you're the only one on the block that didn't have the good sense to take his garbage can to the curb the night before. Well, there's no time now.

Out comes your cell phone, and as you hurtle down the road, coffee in one hand, phone in the other, steering with you knees, you call back to your house.

Ring, ring:

"Hello?"

"Hi, honey, just me. You won't believe this. I forgot to take the garbage out, and I'm late for a meeting. Could you do it for me?"

"I believe it and, yes, I'll do it for you."

"Thanks honey! Love you."

"Love you, too."

Four hours later, a big client you hadn't expected to hear from is in town and would like to see you. You've already made plans to shop for a birthday present for your daughter with your spouse, but this is *important.*

So you call your spouse at work, and in your most apologetic voice explain what has happened this time. The conversation will end something like this:

"Bob's in town, and it's imperative that we get together at noon. Let's go shopping after work."

"It's going to rush us because we have dinner reservations for the family for 7:00 p.m. But if you think there's time, let's do it together then."

"I knew you'd understand honey. Love you."

161

"Love you."

The end of the workday nears, and you're looking forward to spending the evening with your family. Then comes the dreaded phone call. Your service club is working an early evening bingo. They were already understaffed, and now two key members have come down sick. They *really* need you. Now.

You're torn, aren't you? Your common sense says, "Let them work it out themselves. I have plans. Besides, family is more important."

You would be correct in saying that. But in the end, what happens? Your sense of guilt prevails, and you agree to help, just this once. Besides, your daughter will hardly notice you're not there. There will be family and a couple of friends. So you phone your better half and explain the situation. You end with, "I'm sorry this came up now, but you're such a trooper for taking care of everything. I'll make it up to you next time. Love you." "Yeah, right."

What we see here is a whole lot of telling, not much showing, that you love your wife. Let's face it, talk is cheap. If the telling continues and the showing never starts, there's a fifty-one per cent chance in this country that the relationship won't survive.

What on earth, you ask, does this have to do with business? I believe it has everything to do with business. If a husband and wife, the strongest strategic alliance in the world, can't make it work, what hope is there for you and your customers? Are you simply telling them and not showing them that you care? If that's the case, don't be surprised when your customers ask for a divorce from you.

We are forever telling our clients how much we care, how much we value their business. What we usually give, though, is lip service, not Customer Service. Studies show that ninety-one per cent of all businesses have a customer-service theme, customer-satisfaction program, or customer-focused training initiative. Yet only sixteen per cent of

companies state that they're able to r
results.

What goes wrong in between? /
companies rise to national and interna
others flounder, never able to achieve the
set for themselves? I have come to believe
down to one word—care. The companies that really ᵤ.
happen truly care about their customers—then they simply
go about showing, not telling, their customers that they care.

Here's an acronym to help you remember what
CARE is all about:

C ustomer
A ppreciation
R egularly
E xpressed

It's not unusual for me to get a request from someone
high up in a company's food chain to come in and "fix" their
customer service. Invariably this individual is in a panic to
have the seminar or workshop completed because their
image is poor, their service is worse, and it's costing the
company mega-dollars. Inevitably, this individual is tough-
talking, very busy, and will pay big dollars to fix the
problem. Inevitably this person has no intention of
participating in the training themselves—it's their people
that are broken, not them. "Fix it now. Our service stinks.
Tell me how it went."

What's wrong with this picture? These people rarely
see themselves as part of the problem, and it would never
cross their minds that they may be the cause of the problem.
Customer Service can't be "fixed" with a seminar. You can
have your staff attend a customer-service seminar and
nothing will change until the attitude at the top changes and
permeates the culture.

Customer Service isn't a costume. It's not a whizzy
ı. It's not a glitzy advertising campaign. It's an attitude.
_tarts with caring. Southwest Airlines, based in Dallas,
_exas, is a wonderful example of what caring for customers
can do for an organization. From their humble roots in 1967
to today, with more than 300 planes, 30,000 employees, and
$320 million in annual profits, Southwest epitomizes
customer care. No matter the measurement you use, from
safety to on-time arrivals to that pesky luggage arriving at
the correct destination, Southwest leads the field.

Herb Kelliher, CEO of Southwest, talks the talk, but
he also walks the walk. He lives the company's values and
has a buy-in from his people every step of the way. He will
tell you that "we are a service company that happens to own
an airline."

Canadian-based Westjet Airlines has copied every
component of the Southwest business strategy, from flying
only Boeing 737s (saving huge dollars on pilot training) to
specializing in only short hauls, from their ticketless system
to making fun part of every flight. It's the only airline I've
ever flown that boarded passengers by the color of their
socks, jackets, or style of footwear! It is the only airline I've
flown where I have been serenaded by flights attendants and
pilots. At Halloween, they run a promotion whereby people
with the names of Black, Orange, Jack, or Jacks fly for free.
Do they have a winning business acumen? Yes. Targeted
market? You bet. But above all, they truly *care* about their
customers. They make flying with them not just pleasant but
downright *fun*. And they exude caring. Not coincidentally,
Southwest and Westjet are the two most profitable airlines in
North America. They are not the biggest. Only the best.

I traverse the country to facilitate customer-service,
sales and leadership training sessions using Westjet
whenever possible. I would fly to Hamilton and drive a
rental car to Toronto rather than fly directly to Toronto with
another airline before Westjet had Toronto flights. That's
because they *show* me they care.

On a recent early morning flight my two seat companions were brothers, aged twelve and ten, flying for the first time. They boarded just before me and were seen off by their doting mother, who accompanied them as far as she could, then watched their little heads disappear down the jetway.

They were polite youngsters (especially by today's standards) and although they were hesitant to talk with me, they allowed that they were off to visit their grandparents for the last couple of weeks of summer holidays. When offered a drink by the flight attendant, they asked what their choices were. "Juice and pop," she responded.

"Coke, please!" they echoed in unison.

"Do you think it's a little early for coke?" she asked. From the look on her face, I could tell she was regretting mentioning the second choice. You could see the wheels turning as the youngsters pondered the question. Without waiting for the inevitable reply she offered, "I'll tell you what. How about I give you gentlemen the Special Treatment? I'll bring you juice now. I'll even bring you a Coke, if you promise not to open it until you're with your Grandma and Grandpa. Is that fair?"

Special Treatment! WOW! My new companions were suitably impressed. They accepted the offer without hesitation and chattered excitedly about the great deal they just got. For her part, the flight attendant didn't use the guilt-trip line, "What would your Mom say?" She didn't issue a directive, and she didn't cave in. She was totally responsible, and she showed that she cared. I have seen flight attendants on other airlines take the path of least resistance and deliver what was requested. Caring goes beyond doing what the customer wants. It's about doing what is best for them.

If you haven't guessed yet, I am a huge fan of Westjet. A big part of the reason is, they do a lot of the big things right. For instance, if you have no reason to spend half your life in your destination city, you are still able to get a more-than-reasonable fare. No weekend stay required. A lot of my air travel is here today, gone tomorrow, or even here today, gone today, so I appreciate what Westjet does for me there.

When I phone to book a flight, I get to talk to a real human being with a warm and helpful demeanor. To my mind, time, not money, is the currency of the new millennium. We can all go out and make a ton more money, but our ability to grow our time is limited at best. So I appreciate the fact that when I call to book a flight, I don't have to spend any time on hold.

The big things are important, to be sure, but it's the little things that really set Westjet apart, little things that are done by people that care about other people. I was traveling from Saskatoon to Calgary between Christmas and New Year's, the busiest time of year. Now, for all of the nice things WestJet brings to me, they ask for precious little in return. When I arrive at the airport, they ask that I carry picture ID. I have picture ID, but prior to 9/11 had never been asked to produce it. They also give me a confirmation number. There is a good reason for this. Unfortunately, on this day, I had left my confirmation number on my desk. At this busy travel time between Christmas and New Year I showed up at the airport to check in about an hour prior to my flight. You guessed it, there was no record of my booking, although I was sure I had done it. The ticket agent, Diane, was very calm and patient with me, as the line-up behind me started to grow. She looked and looked at her computer screen, but I was apparently non-existent. I thought I would buy another ticket on the spot and straighten the misunderstanding out later. No such luck. The flight was full. I knew the confirmation number was back on my desk and luckily my office was no more than twelve minutes from the airport. I offered to go and find it.

"You would actually leave here to get it?" Diane asked in a shocked voice.

"It's about my only option," was my reply.

"I'm really sorry to have you do that. Are you sure you were booked for this flight?" She queried.

"I've been wrong before, but this time I'm *fairly* certain."

Something must have convinced her, and she continued checking. At this point, though, I was no longer so sure myself, and I headed toward the terminal doors to jump in my car, fully intending to return, confirmation in hand, in plenty of time to catch my flight. As I departed, I noticed that the line-up had grown to include what looked like half the population of Western Canada.

I was at the exit doors, about 200 yards from the check-in counter when I heard "Ron, Ron!"

It was Diane. She chased me down just as I was about to exit the terminal. She had continued working on my problem, allowing the line to grow, until she found me in the computer. My last name had been misspelled.

"Am I ever glad I caught you before you left!" she gasped, breathlessly. Me, too, Diane. Thanks.

It would have been easy for her to holler "Next!," as I raced away, and start to bring that line-up down to a more manageable size. She didn't, though, and that's what makes the difference. My name had been misspelled on my confirmation, where I had missed it, and Diane had the patience and intelligence to figure it out. It was a little thing, but it made a big difference in my day.

For some reason, we seem to think that if we tell our customers what they want to hear, everyone will live happily ever after. What they don't know won't hurt them, we say to ourselves, and we hope that they never find out what it is we are afraid to tell them. We close our eyes and cross our fingers, never for a moment thinking that coming clean, even if it's not what the customer wants to hear, is in everyone's best interest. Keeping the customer informed, in good times and in bad, is a little thing that can render huge results, either positive or negative.

Keeping the Customer in the Loop

"A Tale of Two Experiences"

Since I make my living presenting seminars on Customer Service, I recognize lousy Customer Service when I see it. Conversely, I am also able to recognize excellent Customer Service. Interestingly enough, one seems to amplify the other, especially when they follow closely on each other's heels.

This is a tale of two totally different experiences—one good, one not so good. The biggest difference between the two was that one company chose to keep me in the loop, to keep me informed of what was happening, what had gone wrong, and how they were prepared to fix a problem. The other company chose to treat me like a mushroom—they kept me in the dark and fed me a substance I would prefer not to eat. It is a tale of good news and bad news.

Case One

First, the good news. I was working out of province doing some training for a company with some extreme challenges. I had been on the road all week, was feeling a little beat up, a lot tired, and not very upbeat. I had arranged to meet an old friend for supper and was made even more gloomy when he called my cell after I had arrived at the restaurant to explain that he had been detained at work and wouldn't be able to make our meeting. My goal at this point was to be fed, watered, and sent out the door with the minimum possible interaction. My server showed up at the table, and her smile surpassed ear to ear. This one was bordering on wall to wall! She offered me a beverage before ordering my meal, and I picked one of the brands of beer brewed on site. It arrived in a frosty mug, and, I have to admit, my day was picking up just a little. I placed my order for steak but wasn't wild about the choice of potato. My server recommended a third choice, not on the menu, at no extra charge. It was a small thing, but my appreciation for this place was growing. She also recommended a vegetable, not included with the entree. Could she tell just by looking that I was vegetable deficient? She suggested green beans, one of my favorites. No sooner had I just placed my food order than she re-appeared at the table with a sheepish look on her face—the beer I had ordered wasn't what I received, and under no circumstance would I be charged for it. I hadn't complained, in fact I didn't even know that I had received the wrong product and was already very satisfied with my treatment.

To me, her action represented *total accountability*! How many companies knowingly make errors or provide poor service, all the while hoping the customer doesn't notice, or if they do notice, hoping they don't complain? This was like a breath of fresh air in a polluted world. The error, albeit small, was theirs. They first owned up to the mistake, then responded quickly and massively. This one small act, as much as the great service, and as it turned out, the great food, made my visit memorable. Before my server went off shift, she introduced me to the new server, who proved to be equally professional. Again, I was kept in the loop, not having to wonder who to approach in the absence of my original server. It was a series of small things, minor details, that made the experience work. But then, life is in the details, isn't it?

Case Two
The second tale has very few positives, and that's a shame. It didn't have to be that way. I needed my first pair of progressive eyeglasses, the next generation of bifocals. I spent part of the day shopping at the store owned by the optometric group that I deal with. I had always received good service there but wasn't able to find frames that I liked. I decided to try a new optometrist. Big mistake.

The experience at the new store started well enough. The young lady who offered to help was knowledgeable and patient. I was being fairly selective. Finally, I picked a pair of frames that I thought would do the trick, and the whole atmosphere changed. My salesperson went from helpful consultant to high-pressure salesperson in a heartbeat. I was upsold on everything from scratch-proofing to special cleaner to clip-on sunglasses, all of which I agreed to take. I finalized the purchase and was told that a fifty per cent deposit would be required. Not a problem, I said. I wrote the check for half the amount owing, and was informed that the glasses and clip-on sunglasses would be ready in about two weeks. Not a problem. True to their word, at about the two-week point, I received a phone call stating that the glasses were in. I went to their retail location, and was informed, yes, the glasses are here, but the sunglasses weren't shipped. I was welcome to pay the remainder of the bill, and was informed the sunglasses should arrive within a couple of days. Not a problem. Again, I dutifully wrote my check and headed home.

About two weeks had passed and still no sunglasses and no phone call. My best guess was that the clip-ons had arrived but my salesperson had forgotten or was too busy to phone me. Wrong. When I called them, I was told that they were not in yet. Should just be a couple of days. Not a problem. Two weeks passed, no phone call, no glasses. Again, I initiated contact. By now, they were starting to get mad at *me*! "We told you they're on order, Mr. Morris. When they arrive, we'll call you. It was classic: "Don't call us, we'll call you."

Problem. Anyone that knows me will tell you I am often too patient for my own good, but even my supply of good will was running thin. I was working out of town and didn't have an opportunity to call for three weeks. Every day, I checked my voice mail a minimum of three times, every time expecting a call that the clip-ons were in. It never happened.

By now, I was steamed. My first day back in town I went to their store and tore a strip off the person that sold me the glasses. I made it clear that all I wanted was to know, truthfully, what was going on. She apologized profusely, agreed heartily that the service had been sub-par, and since this was the weekend and the supplier was closed, she would contact the supplier on Monday and update me with the results of that call. Yes, I think you know. Never happened.

Finally, another week later, for the first time, I went over my salesperson's head and contacted the store manager. He listened patiently, assured me this was indeed a rare occurrence, this wasn't the way they normally do business, and what number was I at so he could get right back to me? What does it mean when a person says to you, "I'll get right back to you?" To some people it means minutes, to some people it means hours, to some, days, and to others, weeks. In this case it meant *never!* The manager who was going to get right back to me *never* called. At least I was beginning to understand where the disease came from—it started at the top and spread throughout the branch.

There were three more occasions that I tried to contact the manager. They must have had call display, because each time I called he had "just stepped out." Never did he step back in to call me. Not once.

After a period of four months, a person from the store, with whom I hadn't previously dealt, left a voice mail telling me that my clip-ons had arrived. No explanation. No apology. No anything. I drove down to pick them up. Neither my original salesperson nor the manager were in.

"Here they are. Any questions?" asked the woman behind the counter.

All I wanted to know was what was the reason for the delay.

"I don't know" was her best reply. The tone said, "Do you want them or not? If so, take them; if not, don't bother me."

I left shaking my head, more disappointed than anything else that a company could offer such abysmal Customer Service and remain in business.

Moral of the Story:
If there's a moral here it would be that an act as simple and as small as *keeping the customer in the loop* will build customer loyalty. Ignoring them will earn you a whole lot of "I'll never be back."

Back Off Already!

Try as we may to win our customers over sometimes we are destined for nothing better than the silver medal. It may or may not be our fault. For example a couple intent on an amorous evening open the town would likely care little about their server's name. Ditto people in any form of crisis. Use some discretion and back off, regardless of what your company's policy dictates. Your customers may not verbalize their recognition of your act of kindness, but they will appreciate it. Often they will let you know about their lack of concern about your name, promotions, or special sale items ("Would you like one of our retractable glow-in-the-dark markers for only an additional dollar?") through their words or their body language. Respect that.

It doesn't matter what industry you are in, WOW! Customer Service can separate you from your competitors. What has happened, then, when your staff is well trained in the nuances of dealing with the public, they genuinely care about people, and still there are major blow-ups with customers? Have you totally forgotten a chapter or misinterpreted something so badly that this ranting, cursing, customer threatening to sue you after they cut your heart our with a spoon sees nothing positive about your offering? The sad fact of the matter is that a lot of people go through life like that. They threaten, they complain, they spew venom. You will survive these 'encounters of the worst kind' if you remember that it's not necessarily about you or your service. It's about them and their outlook on life. You only see how these people treat your staff. Believe me, they treat almost every individual they meet in a similar manner.

Every once in a while this will become chronic. The same customer will repeat the same complaint every time they are in your establishment. They will complain about the way the groceries are packed, this time, the last time, and the eight times before that. They will grumble that widget A never fits widget B, and it costs them hours and hours and hours to fix the problem when it's your fault, and when are you going to pay them for that time, they wonder continually? They will exaggerate their claims, they will make a scene, they will be Tasmanian Devils of Poisonous Discontent. They will have you and your staff looking forward to their brightening the room by leaving it.

They leave you with two choices:
1) **Fire them**
2) **Do your level best to WOW! them**

FIRE THEM

What a wonderful world it would be if all customers were created equal and they cared for us as much as we cared for them. Unfortunately, such is not the case. Some require a great degree of handholding, but because they provide us with huge amounts of income or they are pleasant to deal with, we accept their idiosyncrasies. Others may be borderline abusive to us or our staffs, but we give them leeway because they have been good customers historically and may be encountering some short-term personal or business stresses, such as health problems, a marital breakup, cash-flow problems, or the pending loss of a key employee at work. Those things are fair enough, and only the owner of the business can determine whether to fish or cut bait with a customer who fits this category.

Before tossing them overboard you may want to evaluate some meaningful factors, such as whether they pay promptly and how much extra support they require from the standpoint of staffing, returned product, and training, and whether or not they have a detrimental effect on staff morale. Perhaps they refer a lot of business or enhance your company's image through your association with them. Weigh all of your options carefully before you take any drastic measures. Remember from Chapter One that it's easier to keep a customer than to find a new one. These customers can be salvaged.

There are other customers, though, who should be 'dismissed with cause' the second they become problematic. Empower your teams to deal with them in a timely manner that leaves no doubt that a dismissal has occurred. There are no second chances with these former customers. Some reasons for 'dismissal with cause' include but aren't limited to:

a) Customers who ask you to do anything illegal, immoral, or unethical
Customers who request receipts or invoices greater than the amount owing or customers that want a kickback for any reason are not worth the trouble. Your staff is an extension of you, your business, and your reputation. So are your customers. Don't let them for any reason call into disrepute all that you have built.

b) Toxic customers
These are customers whose sole intent, it seems, is to ruin your day. These are the people that, try as you might, you can never satisfy. They bring out not only *their* worst behavior but *your* worst behavior, too. They do pay for the product, usually on time, and they seldom raise their voice. They just complain. And complain. The food was too cold or too hot. The room was too noisy and the TV screen wasn't big enough. The shipment was late and was delivered by a company they didn't like. The seat was too cramped. They were seated by someone they didn't like. The best way to handle them is calmly, but firmly. Never raise your voice, but assume a confident air. Allow that your product or

service may not be perfect. (After all, that's what they've been trying to tell you all along!) If necessary, give them an optional supplier.

"It seems that nothing we do is going to satisfy you. We have tried, but apparently we fall short of your expectations on a regular basis. I am afraid this is as good as we get. It would be better for you if you took your business elsewhere." That's it, end of story. At this point some of them may become apologetic and ask you to reconsider. For the sake of your sanity and your staff's sanity, don't buckle. If you had the courage to confront the complainer, maintain the courage to stay the course. Both you and your staff will benefit. As for the grumpy customer, it is no longer your problem. You haven't lost a customer, you have gained peace of mind.

One thing is certain: your staff will sit up and take notice that you are defending them from the slings and arrows of overly demanding or aggressive customer behavior. Herb Kelliher of Southwest Airlines was once asked if customers are always right. "No, they are not," Kelliher replied heatedly. "And I think that's one of the biggest betrayals of employees a boss can possibly commit. The customer is sometimes wrong. We don't carry those sorts of customers. We write to them and say, 'Fly somebody else. Don't abuse our people'."[12]

c) Any customer who exhibits abusive behavior, either verbally or physically

No one—not you, not your staff—have to put up with that sort of behavior. No job outside of bullfighting, kickboxing or nude skydiving should ask that people put themselves in harm's way to satisfy customers. These are the only people who don't have to be treated with respect. Jettison them now. There may be rare cases where you have to involve a third

---

[12] Kevin Freiberg and Jackie Frieberg , *NUTS!* , (Bard Press, Austin, Texas, 1996) page 268.

party, such as security or the local police. Don't hesitate for an instant.

The same holds true for abusive phone callers. If their language or tone become threatening, inform them politely that you don't have to tolerate that behavior. If they persist, hang up.

DO YOUR LEVEL BEST TO WOW! THEM

As stated earlier in this chapter, in your mind you may be doing everything right, but still there are instances when the ball gets dropped. Maybe your company dropped the ball, or maybe the customer ripped it from your hands. In any event, it is up to you to do your level best to salvage the situation, to WOW! them, and to turn your challenge into an opportunity.

Chapter Seven

Dealing with Difficult Customers

Sign, Sign, Everywhere a Sign

Who isn't familiar with that old cliché: "The customer is always right"? Whoever first made that statement likely had a very small customer base. My experience has been that the vast majority of people that I have dealt with have been wonderful people. They are courteous, understanding, and thoroughly enjoyable company. While they are legion, it is the few, the incensed, and the problematic that stand out in our minds. It matters not where the blame lies. When a customer has passed from the "miffed" stage to the "really pissed" stage to the "ballistic" stage, the last thing you should care about is who was at fault. Thus, the more accurate cliché: "The customer is always the customer."

It doesn't matter, especially to a customer who appears to have gone off the deep end, who is at fault. It may be something that as a company we have done, such as failing to deliver an order on time, or it may be that our customer has just received a threatening letter from the revenue department and is looking for an opportunity to vent. Their prime concern is to have the problem rectified. That, plainly and simply, is their position. It is not about you, it's about them. Your position is to comply with their wishes, no matter who was in the wrong. Don't make the mistake of placing the blame back in the customer's lap, even if you think it's warranted. An upset customer is an upset customer is an upset customer, regardless of whether we did it to them, someone else did it to them or they did it to themselves. A customer with a complaint that appears to have no justification has to be treated with the same respect, care, and responsiveness as the customer whose spaghetti dinner we dropped on their best dress.

There are times, let's face it, that we do it to ourselves. Some customer comes down on us like the wrath of Khan, and we wonder where it comes from. Sometimes we are responsible for setting a negative tone prior to our customer reaching the checkout or even before they have a chance to enter our door. Before we even think about devising a plan to deal with difficult people, let's look first at some of the little things that might irritate them that are caused by us.

Doesn't a warm fuzzy come over you when you are in a gift shop and you are greeted by a sign that says, "You break it, you buy it." A sign like that doesn't make me want to pick up the merchandise and look at the price tag on the bottom. "I'll just leave now to eliminate any chance of breaking anything" is my thought.

Another favorite is "NSF Charge $20." Usually this will be present at a garage or service station. I have to confess, it's been some time since someone has bounced a check on me. Is that what it costs to make it right? These places also often display the checks of the unfortunates that had the bad luck or poor management skills to bounce checks on this upstanding establishment. Isn't it bad enough that these people have suffered the embarrassment of having their bank and possibly their family know that they've screwed up? I know there's a very small percentage of the population that is out to get all they can for as little as they can, and if that means screwing a few merchants over, so be it. Those people are so few and far between, though, that it hardly warrants a sign. In my mind, the NSF sign speaks volumes more about the establishments displaying them than the poor sap that has had his or her bounced check on display for the world to see. One establishment that I drove by went way overboard making their pitiful point. They have a reader board at the front of their property. Instead of using this tool to promote their business, they wrote "Ralph Schicklegruber, please pay your bill." Now, I don't know Ralph personally, nor do I know the circumstances that led to him not paying his bill. I do know, though, that any business that would place such a sign is run by a bitter, vindictive mental midget that I want no part of. You can bet that this is the kind of guy, if he cared enough about Customer Service, would call me to say that his staff is really lousy and could I come in and fix it for the fewest possible dollars? "Oh, by the way," he would likely say, "I won't be there. I have to spend that day thinking of new things to put on my sign so I can insult a few more of my customers." If negative signage is part of your business, take a minute to slip into your customers' shoes. How would you feel entering an establishment that screams of negativity? I thought so. So would your customers.

Another favorite is the "Smile, you're on camera" sign, designed to deter shoplifters at any number of businesses. If you're at all like me, your thought process goes something like this: before you even get through their door, you know they don't trust you and that they'll be watching your every move. What if my shorts bind or I am overcome with an overwhelming need to scratch in a place that shouldn't be scratched on camera? Will I provide hours of uproarious entertainment for a bunch of strangers? For the record, the examples chosen were hypothetical only. The point is, I have a negative feeling about any establishment that displays such a sign and will likely take my business elsewhere. Even if I decide to deal with you, by the time I get to the till, I will resent dealing with you. If you give me a reason, even a small reason to tick me off, I will jump at the opportunity to unload on you, just because you don't trust me. Yes, some people do take it personally.

Restaurants that display the sign "Minimum charge $5 between 11:30 a.m. and 1:30 p.m." are also irksome. You have no qualms about taking what you can get from me the other twenty-two hours a day, but these two hours are sacred. Don't get me wrong, I understand the need to make hay while the sun shines, but there has to be a better way than a sign such as that. These are the restaurants that also have signs that say "Minimum two to a booth," "Pay here," and "No shirt, no shoes, no service." Well, that last one kind of makes sense. Who wants to eat at an establishment with tables crammed with Homer Simpson look-alikes, all sitting around shirtless and shoeless? Still, are we so stupid that we need a sign to remind us of what should be the least acceptable level of etiquette? I swear, one day, just for fun, I'm going to an establishment displaying this sign, and I will arrive with shoes and shirt—but no pants. How long before they put up a new sign? Maybe I'll go with my lawyer, just to make sure I get served!

There are lots of other signs that make us feel equally negative towards the company displaying them:

"No pets."
"No loitering."
"Sampling is considered theft."
"No parking. Violators will be towed."
"Keep off the grass."

Let's do ourselves and our customers a favor and lose the negative signage. While we're at it, we should also eliminate the signs that are meant to bring us bushels of easy sales by tricking our loyal customers. You know the ones I mean:

GOING OUT for BUSINESS SALE

What's up with that? Do we feel that our products or services are so weak that we have to resort to skullduggery to sell them? Or do we feel that our customers are complete morons and wouldn't mind in the least being tricked into buying our inferior products?

My point is simply this: Let's eliminate as much as the negativity as possible for our customers. A sign aimed at chastising the three per cent or less of the population that is "out to get us" is only going to offend the remainder of our customers. It doesn't take much to make our customers walk. They may leave over something as minuscule as an ill-conceived handwritten sign.

182

Forget the Blame Game

If we have been guilty of these transgressions, we can make it right by losing the signage. What happens, though, when the complaint is not of our making, when the customer is clearly in the wrong? There is nothing to be gained by getting into a string of accusations and counter-accusations. If we value this customer, and if we want to retain their business, and even WOW! them, there is a way. It isn't easy, but it can be done. Here's how.

A Formula to Win Over the Angriest Customer

There are times when our customers are out for blood. They could be irate for any number of reasons. What should be an opportunity to build on our customers' loyalty more often than not turns into an exchange that goes sideways or maybe even downhill. Let us, here and now, devise a plan for dealing with these folks so that they want to come back and deal with us time and time again, even after a confrontation.

We usually fail to pick up the ball because we don't have a plan. We try to do the right thing, and in doing so we fall into the trap of escalating the confrontation. We say or do exactly the wrong thing. We have the ability to intensify our irate customer's attitude from miffed to angry to ballistic in scant seconds. And oftentimes we don't even know what it is we have done wrong. People that are new to their customer-service positions normally have the greatest problem overcoming adversity usually because of their lack of experience. But even veterans at serving the public are caught off guard occasionally. It's as though they say, "Here comes someone who looks really mad. I wonder what will fall out of my mouth this time?"

In heated moments like these, what are really 'moments of truth' come off more like 'chances to maximize the damage on both sides.' When a customer is really working us over, our natural instincts call for us to:

a) justify our position, or
b) fight back to the degree we are being attacked.

Neither of these options, other than making you feel good momentarily, are effective. Justifying your position will do nothing to solve the problem at hand and as often as not includes us passing the buck rather than fixing the problem. And as for fighting back, we have lost control and apparently care less for our customer than our wounded ego. If we are in a situation where we are responding in a similar manner as the customer, who is swearing, red faced, and starting to threaten, it's game over. There is a way to turn this situation around, and there is an opportunity to WOW! this person across from you displaying these adversarial tendencies.

Let's look at a formula that will serve you well, no matter your tenure, in any customer confrontation, and will leave you with your dignity and the customer's loyalty intact.

A Win/Win Formula

L
I
S
T
E
N

L *Listen*

very carefully to what your customer is saying to you. As noted earlier, when someone is really giving you the gears, your first two responses are normally to defend and justify your position and to fight back, not necessarily in that order. No matter how much sense these approaches seemingly make to you, neither are the proper responses.

In addition to allowing the customer to vent, you are being given very valuable clues as to what they really perceive the problem to be and how you may go about making it right. The most important of these points, though, is to allow the customer time to vent. Assume an open, non-aggressive stance, with your hands by your sides, and focus on what the customer is saying. It's fine to nod your head from time to time or to utter the odd "uh-huh" or "I see." Beyond that, remain totally silent. Don't even think of saying, "But you don't understand," or "That's not our company policy," or, the granddaddy of them all, "You're wrong!" These short, seemingly harmless phrases are almost guaranteed to make you assault your customer's fist with your nose.

Why is listening so difficult? Perhaps it is because we are used to normal conversation, where the speaking/listening ratio is close to 50:50. We aren't used to active listening, where the speaking/listening ratio changes to 20:80. Luckily, active listening is, in fact, a skill that can be learned, and, for my money, well-developed active listening skills are likely the most useful communication tools you can possess. There is a huge difference between passive and active listening. On which side of the chart are you most likely to appear?

PASSIVE LISTENING	ACTIVE LISTENING
No notes being taken	Might make some notes
Quickly forget what you've been told. You are just waiting for your turn to talk	Hold concentration
Poor eye contact. Disconnected, or glaring	Continual "soft" eye contact
Posture reflects "who cares?" attitude	Straight posture, but non-threatening
Never asks questions	Waits until customer is done venting, then asks appropriate questions

There are key benefits to active listening. In addition to letting the customer blow themselves out, you will understand what that red-faced person across from you is trying to say. It will help you decide which course of action is best, and, as we will explore next, it will help your prejudices and emotions from getting in the way. The pitfalls that get in the way of active listening include making assumptions about what the speaker is about to say, because that's what happened last time, getting impatient for your turn to talk, and allowing mental or physical distractions to take your focus off of the speaker.

Do your best to be an active listener. It will pay dividends from a stress-relief standpoint and help you build from a bad situation.

I *In-mote*

Before you go running to your dictionary to determine if there is such a word, let me save you the time. The word is a hybrid, and it reflects that you keep *in* check your *emotions*. The worst thing that can happen is to get caught up in the emotional frenzy that is fueling your customer's passion.

While you are attentively listening, remain emotionally detached.

Don't take it personally

Our emotions will bubble to the surface when we feel that the attack is targeted towards us. It's hard not to feel some sort of rebound anger when the customer is venting their wrath on us. The most valuable piece of information I could offer to you in this entire formula is not to take the attack personally. Remind yourself that the customer is angry with the product, with your company, or perhaps even with a policy that gets in the way of good Customer Service. You are merely a convenient outlet which allows them to vent. So, don't let this one-sided volatile interaction ruin your day, your week, or your life. The next person you have to deal with doesn't know and doesn't care about the personal hell you just went through. Like the last customer, the next customer wants you to make them feel as if they are the only person in the universe. So do your level best to remain emotionally calm, at least on the outside, and never take it personally.

Don't be prejudiced towards an angry customer

Once an ugly situation is underway, we will search our brains frantically for a similar experience to reference. In almost every case, the reference will be a negative one. Once that happens, we have instantly developed an opinion as to the outcome of our current situation. We have also developed an opinion of the person who is giving us grief. "What a jerk" or "what an unreasonable moron" are examples of mild phrases that creep into the back of our mind. Often we think in terms a lot stronger (and less printable) than those. And guess what? Once we have developed this opinion, once we have built this prejudice, we will treat our antagonist in exactly the manner in which we see them. Or we may see the same customer approach us that gave us the gears the last time we saw them. Instinctively we

187

clench our teeth, our heartbeat quickens, and we begin to perspire. The downward spiral has begun even before they have said a word. We are pre-judging the outcome of this person's visit. Don't think they can't feel the negative vibe you hold for them. If you don't keep an open mind, this interaction has a far greater chance of ending in disaster than it does of ending on a positive note.

Here's an example. I have fought an ongoing battle with my weight for the last twenty years, with my weight holding the upper hand. I could be described as a short, fat guy. In my youth and far as into my thirties, I tried to at least stay active to keep my weight in three digits. In recent years though, my hips deteriorated to the point where physical activity was virtually impossible. Having viewed a number of ads for weight-loss products, I thought I would inquire into some good programs at a local health-food store. Now, I am not a person who believes that a magic pill was about to solve all my fitness woes, but I hoped against hope that there was a product that would at least help me from growing to gargantuan proportions.

The interaction went exactly like this:

Me: *Good Morning!*

Clerk: (Furiously stocking shelves) *Hello.*

Me: *I was wondering, are there any products that you could recommend that would help me lose weight?*

Clerk: (Giving me a quick once over while continuing to furiously stock shelves) *Well, I can think of three things that would help you.*

Me: *Three products?*

Clerk: *No. Three things you can do. First, cut down the amount of red meat you eat.*

Me: *Oh, thanks. I had read that and have been able to do it with some success.*

Clerk: (Eyeing me suspiciously) *Second, drop the snacks, and introduce more grains into your diet.*

Me: *Makes sense. I have actually developed a liking for bagels.*

Clerk: (Hands on hips, scolding) *The third thing is you should try to get some exercise.*

Now at this point she didn't say, "You fat pig," but that's what I heard loud and clear.

Me: *Thanks.*

Clerk: (Recommencing to furiously stock shelves as I left the store for good) *My pleasure.*

My guess was, there were a few short fat guys and girls in recently looking for a quick fix, and her prejudice said, "Here comes another one. If I don't blow him off, I'll never get these shelves stocked." To that end, she was successful. That was ten years ago. My battle of the bulge continues. Some days I do better than others. I spend a lot of money on vitamins and selected herbs. Not at that store. Ever.

Nothing in the world will make a prejudice towards a customer or a situation go away completely. But at least recognize it, and with a partially open mind and a smile on your face, complete the interaction as quickly and painlessly as possible, then move on.

S *Sympathize*

To this point, you have been fairly quiet, allowing the customer to vent, listening carefully for clues that will offer a solution and keeping your emotions on the back burner. In almost all cases, the customer has now blown themselves out. "If there is no fight," they say to themselves, "why am I making such a fuss?" Why indeed? While you are still in a conflict situation, there need no longer be a confrontation. The basis to every relationship, be it business or personal, is trust. By sympathizing with the customer's plight, you have built the basis for trust. By no means does this mean going over to their side and bashing your company for their shortcomings. All it means is that you show understanding, and you can relate to their plight. Here are a few sympathetic phrases to show the customer that you care:

"You certainly are upset. If I were in your shoes, I would be too."

"This has to be very frustrating for you."

"I understand how you must feel."

"I'm sorry this happened."

Oftentimes I am challenged on this last phrase during my seminars. "As soon as you say 'I'm sorry,' some of my students tell me, you are admitting that you are in the wrong." That may well be. If that's the case, so be it. Our objective here is to win over an upset customer, not win a pissing contest. Does that mean that the customer is always right? Not in my books. There are instances when I think you have to fire your customer (Chapter Six); however, in the heart of a heated debate is not the right time. But it doesn't hurt either side if the customer is perceived as being right. Remember our goal is to win them over, not be proven right. What a hollow victory that would be.

T *Thank Complaining Customers*

Some of you at this point, especially the Driver personality types, are set to put the book down. These people will think, "First I have to say I'm sorry, and now this nut case wants me to *thank* people for giving me grief? Ethel, take this book to the used-book store!" Before you do that, let me explain why this step is important in the process. Industry standards tell us that for every person that bothers to voice a complaint, there are twenty-three others that feel the same complaint but are either non-combative or have little confidence in your problem-solving abilities. These people pose a grave danger to your business. These are the people that will tell their friends and family about your lousy service, but they won't tell you. Statistics tell us that unhappy customers will tell between eight and sixteen people about their negative experience. That, however, was before the Internet came into play. Now, with little effort, these same people are able to tell thousands of people at a time how they feel about your Customer Service.

Create Complaining Customers

If twenty-three to twenty-six people feel a complaint that only one verbalizes, doesn't it make sense to have a few more complaints, so you can see what the issues really are? Customers that care enough to complain are not a nuisance, they are a godsend. They give you a concrete idea as to where you've gone wrong. Between the two of you, you can set about fixing the problem. Customers that care enough to complain allow you to red-flag areas of your business that you may not have been aware were hazardous to your business's health. Customers that care enough to complain are your best friends. Thank them often, and thank them sincerely. Try saying, "Thank you for bringing that to my attention. I really wasn't aware it was a problem until you brought it up."

You should also make it easy for your customers to lodge a complaint. If you do it in the right way, they will see themselves as helping you on the way to WOW! Customer Service. My personal favorite is the old-fashioned suggestion box, which is making a comeback in a large number of industries. The section on Feedback Standards in Chapter Three will also help you to identify problem areas.

E *Extend a Solution*

While you and your customer may not yet be ready for a hug, if you have followed the steps outlined above, your customer will be convinced by now that you have their best interests at heart. Now is your opportunity to make it right. The conversation at this point is normalizing, at a close to 50:50 speaking/listening ratio. Now is the time to ask some pertinent questions to ensure that you offer the right solution. Let's face it, when a customer feels hard done by, they will occasionally exaggerate to make their point. Don't hold this against them. It is merely human nature at work. Make sure the questions you ask are open-ended, and non-accusatory. As at the beginning of the process, listen carefully to their answers.

At this point you can go one of two ways:

1) **You can offer a solution based on the information you have gleaned from listening, or**
2) **You can ask the customer what they think the best solution would be.**

Don't hesitate to use the second option. If you have followed these steps, you will be surprised how little it takes to make it right. It may be something as little as an apology. Nine people out of ten will offer a solution that you can not only live with but that may be less than you were prepared to offer. Bear in mind that one in ten will not offer a solution that is anywhere near fair. They will ask for the moon, the stars, and the sky. By noon. Gift wrapped. Having come this far, you can still win even with these people. Never come back at them with a negative like "I'm sorry, but that solution is out of the question." Rather, approach it from a positive standpoint, such as "Here's what I *can* do." This type of person is likely trying you on for size. They will understand your approach and will more often than not accept your solution.

Whatever the agreed-upon solution, however, make sure to perform as you said you would. Now is a time to underpromise and overdeliver. If you know it will take two days to solve the problem, tell the customer it will take four. When the problem is solved in half the expected time, your customer will be WOW!ed.

N *Nullify the Damage*
A study done by the *Harvard Business Review* indicated that in some cases customers are more loyal following an

altercation with a company than if no altercation took place at all. While this isn't always possible, it should always be your goal. There are two ways to nullify the damage:

1) **Do More Than the Customer Expects—Respond Massively and Rapidly**
2) **Follow up**

What Does the Customer Expect?

The customer doesn't expect you to poke the offending customer-service representative on the nose. They do expect, though, to be taken seriously and to be treated with respect. You will do yourself no favors if you gloss over what has just transpired as though it isn't important, because to your customer it is a big deal. They may want restitution or compensation, and they will certainly want the problem rectified so it doesn't happen again. Above all, the customer wants to be listened to. These few points are the minimum standards you should apply in customer-conflict situations. These few points are a good start, but by themselves they won't nullify the damage done in a conflict situation. So, what's next?

1. Do More Than the Customer Expects—Respond Massively

Now that we have a good handle on the customer's expectations, let's set out to WOW! them. When I say respond massively, I don't mean you have to give away the ranch. Anything you do over and above the already mentioned reasons will be seen by the offended customer as huge. If, for example, you own a men's wear store, include a pair of dress socks to calm the customer. A restaurant that I went to gave a coupon for a free dessert after my dinner companion complained about the portions being too large! It doesn't have to cost you an arm and a leg, but the customer will see you going out of your way to make amends.

2. Do More Than the Customer Expects—Respond Rapidly

Statistically speaking, there is much to be gained by responding to a customer's complaint immediately. As you will recall from Chapter Three on Standards, fifty-four per cent of customers will come back to you following a conflict if you solve the problem. A full eighty-two per cent will come back if the problem is solved quickly. If ever there was a great reason to empower employees to make their own decisions as to how to respond to customer complaints, this is it. As a business owner or manager, you get to retain almost thirty per cent more of your customer base. What does that equate to in dollars and cents?

3. Follow up

This, more than anything else will set you apart from your competitors. Whether or not the fault for the altercation lies with you, the customer will appreciate that you are being accountable. After you think the problem has been solved, don't assume all is well just because you haven't heard from your customer—they may have given up on you and, rather than telling you, are telling their friends and relatives how bad your service is. A quick phone call, e-mail, or personal visit from you will bring any existing problems to the surface and will establish you as a person of integrity. These are the actions that will build loyalty and have your customers sending you referrals by the dozen. That is when you have reached the Power of WOW!

Not All Customers Are Created Equal

More and more companies are being selective about who they want to deal with. Not all customers are created equal. There are those that fit our niche and those that don't. Let me give you an example. If you are the owner of an alternative night club, where the music's lyrics, when intelligible, are profane and the noise, er, music is played at three billion decibels, you won't much care if I, as a fifty-plus person ask you to turn the music down. If however, you are the owner of an upscale restaurant and my wife and I, out for an intimate dinner are offended by a table of boisterous, drunken buffoons, you are much more likely to pay attention to my request. I am the person you want in your establishment, not the louts. No matter your industry, you have some consumers that are made for you, and you for them. That is the nature of business, and it's perfectly normal to try to appeal to a certain segment or demographic. As long as the people you dismiss are done so with respect, you will be fine. Besides being the right thing to do, word of mouth won't come back to haunt you. Remember, even the fifty-plus guy who wandered into your alternative night club may have some influence with people you would like to connect with. Be careful how you let your customer go.

It is how you and your staff handle stresses, such as handling difficult customers, and how you set and live up to your standards that will define you as a Power of WOW! company. It is the way you hire and listen to and respect your staff that will determine whether or not they say "WOW!" about being part of your team. These are the true measures of success, not merely how your profit and loss statement reads. As stated earlier, Customer Service is an attitude. That is true. But it's more than that, it's a journey. Our success isn't measured merely by the bottom line, but rather how we arrived there. Wrong process, wrong result. Right process, right result. Let's put it all together.

Chapter Eight

Putting It All Together

As we discussed in Chapter Three, the Power of WOW! Customer Service Formula is:

S + T x Ex =POW!
Standards + Teamwork x Execution =
Power of WOW!

We have devoted ample time learning about how to surpass customers' expectations by delivering more than they expect and by setting tough but attainable *standards* that are measurable and consistent. We found out about how to hire properly, and how to retain great staff. We determined how to treat *team* members so that they can accomplish all that they can, and our teams can function in a spirit of harmony and energy with a collective goal of WOW!ing the customer.

In short, you have learned all you need to know to transform satisfied customers into loyal customers by providing Power of WOW! Customer Service. If you took everything to heart that you have learned in these pages, you would really have no need to send staff to another customer-service seminar or to read another book on the subject. Don't get me wrong—that's not what I'm suggesting. But if everything you read here is applied, you will develop a WOW! Customer Service culture, and you will lead your industry. It is all here. However, while my work is almost done, yours is just beginning. For you, the transformation from concept to reality is upon you. What will you do now to *execute* your customer-service plan? This is where great customer-service plans break down—in the execution phase. To help you ensure that your plan succeeds, following is an outline designed to help you get on track and stay on track. Customer Service is always a work in progress. Someone, hopefully you, is always raising the bar. These exercises are a starting point only. Revisit your customer-service program a couple of times per year. Make the necessary changes, always striving to improve, if only slightly, on your existing service.

Customer-Service Outline

Standards

1. Feedback Standards

Implement a minimum of three methods over the next twelve months from the following list to garner feedback from your customers

 a) Face-to-face meetings with customers at your place of business
 b) Complaint mechanisms, such as a complaint or suggestion box
 c) Advisory boards made up from your customer base
 d) Focus groups either on site by you and your staff or of site facilitated by a professional
 e) Hot lines
 f) Conferences and conventions

2. Recovery Standards

What steps will you take to win back the customers' loyalty after you have offended them? Set standards for both minor and a major miscues. Be well prepared in advance of a fumble. It may or may not be your doing, but it will happen. If possible, assign a low dollar value to the standard. Remember, Power of WOW! is about more than money. It's about doing more than the customer expects.

Steps to take

1 _____

2 _____

3 _____

4 _____

5 _____

3. Image Standards

Pick two areas from the following list where you feel your image could use a little fine tuning:

1. Master/Mistress of Details
2. Ability to anticipate customer needs
3. Can-do attitude
4. Mental toughness
5. Consistency in results
6. Product knowledge
7. Integrity
8. Making a difference in peoples' lives
9. Personal excellence
10. Respect
11. Reputation
12. Work ethic

Work on only one of these components at a time. Do so for twenty-one days, since that's how long it takes to form a new habit.

4. Client Communication Standards

A Amiable	**B** Expressive
Clothes: Trendy, fashionable, leaning towards conservative. May wear brand-name clothing. Overall, will tend to wear what their peers are wearing. Car: Popular vehicle, potentially a former "Car of the Year," not too showy or sporty. It could be a station wagon or mini-van. Office: Feels warm. Family Pictures, kid's art, plants, possibly piped-in music. Their business cards will be front and center on their desk, maybe in a funky holder, like a ceramic purse or baseball glove. **Hot Buttons: Relationships, acceptance, and non-confrontation.**	Clothes: Flamboyant, flashy. Their clothing will make a statement. It may border on loud. They will be accessorized with dangling and/or showy jewelry. In business, they will appear crisp. Car: Likely two-door, sporty, vibrant color. Will have toys, bells, and whistles. A great sound system is a must. Office: "A Shrine to Them." Pictures of themselves with famous people, or accomplishing feats. Plaques, awards and designations. May have trendy art or motivational posters. **Hot Buttons: Image, willingness to take risks, need to have fun and be the center of attention at work or play. They have an opinion.**
C Analytical	**D** Driver
Clothes: Practical, functional, conservative. May be mix and match. Car: Functional, economical, and likely conservative. It may well be paid for. Office: Organized chaos. There will be charts, graphs, and little piles of paper everywhere. Touch those piles at your own risk. **Hot Buttons: Facts, data, information, numbers, and a need to be correct.**	Clothes: Conservative, good quality. Little in the way of accessories. Car: Like their clothing, it will be conservative in color and could be a four-door sedan or SUV. Office: Neat, well organized, possibly Spartan. **Hot Buttons: Control, results, bottom line, opinion.**

Evaluating Service Quality

The work of customer-service researchers Berry, Parasuraman, and Zeithaml tell us that across industries, and across the nation, customers had five factors that they used to evaluate service quality. It doesn't matter if you are in retail, health care, or hospitality. Ditto for automotive, safety, or manufacturing. The five most important factors that your customers value are, in descending order[13]:

1. **Reliability**
2. **Responsiveness**
3. **Assurance**
4. **Empathy**
5. **Tangibles**

Let's look at each of these factors to determine where and how they fit into your business.

1. Reliability
Reliability is not much more than doing what you say you will do. It also means doing it on time, doing it right, and doing it right the first time. A customer of a restaurant expects a good meal at a fair price. If you serve your customer a salad with a tarantula playing hide and seek in the spinach or you make grandiose promises that you can't deliver on, you may be perceived as less than reliable.

An airline's offer is to get you from one point to another, safely and on time, with your luggage waiting for you at the carousel. Lots of airlines specialize in two out of three, and some airlines seem able to deliver on only one of these. These airlines are deemed to be unreliable.

---

[13] A. Parasuraman, L. Berry, V. Zeithaml, "Servqual," (*Journal of Retailing, Spring,* 1988) pages 12-40.

The wonderful thing about reliability is that it fits under the umbrella of integrity. If you do only what you say you will do, statistically you are already better than sixty per cent of the businesses out there. Broken promises, late deliveries, and shoddy goods will get you a lot of loneliness. Doing what you said you would do, though, makes you a businessperson of integrity, a person who delivers and who stands above the crowd.

2. Responsiveness

When you see a customer puzzling over a price or a product, approach them immediately and offer to help. That's responsiveness. An elderly shopper at Ukrop's Super Markets in Richmond, Virginia, was spotted by company president James Ukrop holding and closely examining a large pineapple. Noticing the quizzical expression on her face, he approached the woman and made it clear that the store would be happy to cut the pineapple in half. Happily, she accepts. She tells him about the wonderful shopping experience at Ukrop's. That is building loyalty through responsiveness. Many companies that I work with have implemented a 'ten/ten' program: the employees will greet the customer within ten seconds of sighting them, or will offer to help if they are within a ten-foot radius. Too many times staffers will race on by a customer sporting a confused look or obviously having difficulty finding a product. These staffers hope against hope that the customer will find what they are looking for on their own or just go away to a place where they won't make the staffer's life a living hell by forcing them to do their job. Those staff members should be careful what they wish for. There's not a lot of job security with a business that has no customers.

Responsiveness plays a huge role in problem-solving as well. As stated earlier, companies and individuals that respond to problems massively and rapidly have a customer base that doesn't waver in its loyalty. The key is speed.

Handle the problem proactively, on the spot, immediately, and good things will be yours.

3. Assurance
This reflects on your ability to send the message to your customers that you are trustworthy, competent, confident, and deserving of their business. A great example of assurance is exhibited by Nissan. Every employee, regardless of department or position must attend a six-day "boot camp," which covers every facet of the business. When employees return from camp, they are able to answer customer questions without putting the customer through to a salesperson. Imagine the assurance this gives a customer or potential customer when their query is answered by the receptionist or a young person in car preparation. "Imagine," they must think, "if their front-line people are this smart, I can hardly wait to meet their technical experts!"

4. Empathy
Empathy could best be described as the level of understanding, caring, and individual attention you give to your customers. This could be described as a 'warm fuzzy.' Companies have to develop the ability to make customers feel the product or service has been developed just for them. When things go wrong for the customer because of something you have done, be prompt with an "I'm sorry." People hearing that powerful phrase feel that the company has empathy for them. Those two powerful words indicate that you regret what has happened to upset your customer. It is *not* an admission of guilt, and if it were, so what?

5. Tangibles
This is where companies tend to spend the majority of their time, money, and energy. Tangibles include our buildings, our company vehicles, and our uniforms. They also include our stationery, from invoices to letterhead, from promotional brochures to envelopes. While these things are essential to

establishing our brand, our customers see fit to grace them with only the number-five spot in things that are most important to them. Our sense of pride and professionalism should be sufficiently enticing to keep our 'things' in order. The interesting thing is that price, often thought of as a key component in attracting customers, is not even in the top five. My experience has taught me that the companies that think of price as hugely important to the success of their customer-service programs are most likely lacking in one or more of the other areas that customers value. Price may play a roll in WOW!ing customers, but that role is diminished if customer loyalty is our aim.

A Matter of Perspective

Let's wrap it up as we began, with a story. As with the Civil War story, I wasn't there, but people tell me the story is true nonetheless. There were two young men from the prairies who had never seen the Rockies. Their goal was to undertake a two-week camping holiday in Banff National Park, but there was a problem. Bears had been wreaking havoc in the campgrounds. Safety had become a serious issue, but our heroes were determined to experience the mountains first-hand, so they decided to learn as much as they could on 'bear proofing.' They started with their local library, where they checked out and vigorously studied every book possible on the topic. Their confidence grew, but still there was more to learn. Their next stop was the Internet, where they researched every 'bear-proofing' article on every search engine. Finally, after weeks of study, they set out in their pickup truck to experience their vacation of a lifetime. Upon their arrival in Banff, they decided to undertake one final safety measure. They attended the seminar put on by one of the park wardens on dos and don'ts when in bear country. At long last they were ready, and they trooped deep into the mountains.

Their first night of camping found one of our heroes cooking over a roaring campfire, while the other fellow was nowhere to be seen. Suddenly, from behind a bush came an earth-shaking roar. A monstrous grizzly bear emerged from behind the bush, with a head a large as a television and razor-sharp teeth and claws. The beast approached the campfire menacingly, but our prairie boy was unflappable. He recalled instantly every sentence he had read, every related story, every example of what to do in case of a bear attack. First he dumped the coffee pot and fry pan that were warming over the fire, and began to bang them together furiously. The bear stopped, but showed no signs of retreat. Next, our hero yelled and screamed as loud as he could, while he continued with the pots and pans, hoping to intimidate the bear. Still, the bear held its ground, showing no signs of retreat. At this point our hero, looking for some backup, glanced over at the tent, where his partner was lacing his sneakers in a frenzied manner.

Campfire boy shouted "Hey, Seth! Don't you remember all of our training? Don't you remember that you can't outrun a bear?"

To which our friend in the tent, now fully laced and starting out at a trot, called over his shoulder, "I don't have to outrun the bear. I just have to outrun you!"

So it is in Customer Service. You just have to outrun your competitor.

Lace up those sneakers.

Recommended Reading

Nuts! Southwest Airlines' Crazy Recipe for Business and Personal Success
by Kevin and Jackie Freiberg

Best Practices in Customer Service
A compilation, edited by Ron Zemke and John H. Woods

Customer Centered Growth—Five Proven Strategies for Building Competitive Advantage
by Richard Whiteley and Diane Hessan

Customer Satisfaction is WORTHLESS—Customer Loyalty is Priceless
by Jeffrey Gitomer

The Service Profit Chain
by Heskett, Sasser, and Schlesinger

Customer Service For Dummies
by Karen Leland and Keith Bailey

First, Break all the Rules
by Marcus Buckingham and Curt Coffman

Love 'Em or Lose 'Em
by Beverly Kaye and Sharon Jordan-Evans

Order Form

I wish to order additional copies of:

_____ Power of WOW! Customer Service

Name: _____

Shipping Address: _____

_____

$19.95 each (Canadian) or $16.00 (US)
plus $2.00 for tax, shipping and handling.

Payment should be made to:
Ron Morris Seminars
111 Makaroff Road
Saskatoon, SK
S7L 6R5

ronmorrisseminars@sasktel.net